THE ATONEMENT

by

J. W. C. WAND

Canon and Treasurer of St Paul's, formerly Bishop of London

LONDON

S · P · C · K

1963

First published in 1963
by S.P.C.K.
Holy Trinity Church
Marylebone Road
London N.W.1

Made and printed in Great Britain by
William Clowes and Sons, Limited, London and Beccles

© J. W. C. Wand, 1963

ACKNOWLEDGEMENTS

Extracts from the Revised Standard Version of the
Holy Bible, copyrighted 1946 and 1952, from the
New English Bible, New Testament, copyright
1961, Oxford and Cambridge University Presses,
and from the Book of Common Prayer, which
is Crown copyright, are included in this book by
permission.

Contents

1. Introduction   1

2. The Example of Love   12

3. The Concept of Victory   23

4. Substitution   34

5. Transaction   44

6. Satisfaction   54

7. Vicarious Penitence   63

8. Mystical Union   72

9. The Atonement To-day   81

NOTE

The reader who is not interested in mere words as such would be well advised to skip pages 2–5.

1

Introduction

ATONEMENT is the heart of the Christian religion: it is its very core and centre. All the more curious is it that in the Church there is no officially received doctrine of the Atonement. The fact is accepted as fundamental: the explanation is open to discussion.

This open-mindedness as to the means does not imply that the Christian is left without guidance in his thinking about so fundamental a matter. On the contrary, as we shall see, the subject has occupied some of the greatest minds down the centuries, and they have left their views on record for all to see and endeavour to understand. It was inevitable that these views should have been conceived very largely in reaction against each other. One scholar's thought-provoking view has led another to say "Yes, but . . .", and he has evolved a new view out of his partial disagreement.

Some students have spoken as if these different views were mutually contradictory, as if they entirely excluded each other. That is not so. It is probable that there is some element of truth in each of them and that we can only get the whole truth if we try to hold them in balance together. The Atonement is like a precious jewel, which is so large that you can only see properly one facet at a time. To get a sufficient idea of it you have to turn it round in your hand and see each facet in turn.

That is what we must try to do in this book. We must examine each view in turn, not thinking that one will cancel out the others, but trying to recognize the truth in each one and hold it in the mind until we can mentally see all round the doctrine and comprehend its marvellous beauty as a whole.

We begin by trying to understand what the word itself means. If we take it to pieces, we see that it falls into three self-explanatory syllables: at-one-ment. This analysis gives us a perfectly good sense. Atonement means making man at one with God. It is an event, or series of events, by which man and God are reconciled with each other. Of course that implies that they needed to be reconciled, that they were previously estranged from each other. Christian teaching confirms that a barrier has indeed been raised between them by man's sin. In this book we must simply take that for granted. The subject of sin is treated elsewhere in this series.

The doctrine of atonement in all its forms teaches that the barrier is removed in Christ—how, is the precise point under discussion.

In the meantime we must examine the meaning of atonement in the Bible, which, after all, is the source from which all our ideas come. In the Old Testament the word for "atone" is *kaphar*. It may be used in two senses as one looks either to God's side or to man's side of the barrier. If the gaze is directed towards God, "to atone" means "to propitiate", that is, to appease, conciliate, or render favourable. If, however, the direction is manwards, the meaning is "to expiate", that is, to make reparation or satisfaction for. It is disputed which is the original meaning but both are found in the Old Testament.

What is the actual root meaning of *kaphar* scholars despair of finding out. It is used in two senses, to cover or to wipe away. The cognate word *kopher* is used in the non-liturgical sense of "compensation". Naturally the form of the word most commonly used for atonement, *kipper*, is found most frequently in the legal books of the Pentateuch. It is used in the Old Testament especially of compensation for the taking

2

of human life. This most serious crime can be atoned for either by forfeiting other human life or lives (2 Sam. 21.1-9; Deut. 32.39-43; Ex. 32.30-5), or by surrendering the life of cattle (Deut. 21.6ff), or even by sacrifice, as exemplified by the contrary case of Eli's sons (1 Sam. 3.14).

In the priestly writings the word is used most frequently in connection with the established system of sacrifices. Lev. 17.11 states that it is the blood that makes atonement through the life. It was believed that the soul or life resided in the blood (perhaps because newly spilt blood would "smoke" in the air). Thus when the victim was killed and its blood shed, its life was given to God. Together with the idea of compensation went the twin ideas of purification and sanctification. These were all combined in the impressive ceremonies of the Day of Atonement as described in Lev. 16. According to Num. 15 atonement can only be effected for sins committed unwittingly. For sins committed "with a high hand", that is, deliberately, there appears to be no possibility of atonement (cf. Num. 15.30).

In the Septuagint (the Greek version of the Old Testament) the general idea is represented by two words *katharmos* and *hilasmos*, the former implying cleansing or purification and the latter appeasement of gods, demons, or even the dead. The appropriate verbal form of the latter word is used in Luke 18.13—"God be merciful to me a sinner"—and Heb. 2.17—the high priest "expiates" the sins of the people. It appears that a word which originally had implied an influence exercised by man upon God had by New Testament times come to imply an action of God upon men. The substantive form of the verb (*hilasmos*) appears twice in the first epistle of St John, first in 2.2—Jesus is the "expiation" for our sins—and again in 4.10—God sent his Son to be the expiation for our sins.

A word closely associated with the foregoing terms is that used for the "mercy-seat" (*kapporeth, hilasterion*) above the ark of the covenant in the Temple (Ex. 25.20). There God promised to meet with Moses, and from between the two cherubim that stood one on either side of the seat he would

3

speak with him (Ex. 25.22). This mercy-seat occupied a specially important place in the ceremonial of the Day of Atonement. It became the most important object in the shrine (1 Chron. 28.11), and was looked upon as the place where God appeared in the cloud to his ministrant (Lev. 16.2).

The mercy-seat is not to be regarded as any mere cover or lid of the ark. It was not in fact an essential part of the ark at all. It was something added. The Septuagint describes it in Ex. 37.6 as an addition ("above" or "from above") that is, for atonement. In 1 Chron. 28.11 it is sufficiently important for the room where the ark is placed to be known as the "house of the mercy-seat", and everyone knows of the ceremonies of blood-sprinkling with which it was associated on the Day of Atonement.

In fact the mercy-seat is regarded not only as a symbol of atonement but as part of the actual means by which atonement is attained. So much is this the case that St Paul's use of the word in Rom. 3.25 has provided commentators with a well-known crux: "Christ Jesus, whom God set forth to be a propitiation, through faith, by his blood." (R.V.) The word translated "propitiation" is really *hilasterion*, "mercy-seat". The question has been raised whether Christ is here being likened to the actual piece of furniture or to the victim whose blood was sprinkled on it. The latter interpretation can be dismissed, since the thought of an actual victim is not uppermost in the passage. On the other hand it seems likely that the phrase "by his blood" is to be taken with *hilasterion* rather than with "through faith", that is to say the punctuation should be as given in the Revised Version above. The picture in Paul's mind is thus seen to be the mercy-seat bespattered with blood. This is the atonement, the point at which God and man are reconciled. The New English Bible surrenders the picturesque symbolism in order to bring out the meaning in a more matter-of-fact way: "God designed him to be the means of expiating sin by his sacrificial death, effective through faith."

For Paul the mercy-seat is not something intended to change God from anger to mercy but a place where grace

4

and righteousness meet. Christ by the shedding of his blood has been made a substitute for the sinner and righteousness is satisfied. The sinner who by faith recognizes this substitution is brought to self-judgement and penitence, and is thus open to the reception of God's forgiving grace. So God demonstrates his justice, both in overlooking the sins of the past and in acquitting any man who puts his faith in Jesus (Rom. 3.26).

To consider now the *idea* of atonement (as distinct from the word) in a little more detail. It should be realized that, as Driver points out in the *Encyclopedia of Religion and Ethics*, the idea conveyed by the word in the Bible is not that of modern English. When we use the word in common speech we imply reparation or expiation. In the Bible, however, it means "reconciliation". Driver reminds us that this was the idea behind the word in Shakespeare's time, and he quotes *Othello* (4.1), "I would do much to atone them", that is, to reconcile them. That is no doubt why on the one occasion when "atonement" occurs in the Authorized Version of the New Testament (Rom. 5.11) the Revised Version changes it to "reconciliation". On that occasion, however, the translation is from the Greek, *katallagē*. Obviously the two ideas are closely linked, for when expiation has been made reconciliation becomes possible. This applies even to the land in which a crime is committed: "Blood pollutes the land, and no expiation can be made for the land, for the blood that is shed in it, except by the blood of him who shed it." (Num. 35.33, R.S.V.)

This ordinance is clearly related to the *lex talionis* (an eye for an eye and a tooth for a tooth) which lies behind so much of the Mosaic law. But the necessity for actual equality of retribution was in many instances replaced by that of a ritual satisfaction, the blood of an animal victim taking the place of a human death. Indeed it has been suggested that the word *kaphar* in its Assyrian form always had ritual associations and that these associations were introduced together with the word into the Hebrew language.

However that may be, it is certain that, whatever the law may have been, the principle of commutation (or offering of some other compensation in place of a human life) was observed in practice among the Hebrew people. This choice might be dictated by economic values or by ritual necessity, but in either case it helped to put a stop to the blood feud which was evidently practised in early Israel as in other semi-barbaric circles. A further advance came when it was realized that to readjust relations with God something more than ritual atonement was necessary: the outward offering must reflect the inner change or penitence of the heart.

This is the idea that lay behind the fully developed Jewish practice of sacrifice. There is no need, therefore, for us to go into the various types of sacrifices or into the details of the ceremonies of the Day of Atonement. Having established the Old Testament principle of expiation combined with propitiation we can go on to consider the teaching of the New Testament.

Here we have to be clear again in which of two senses we are using the word atonement. The tendency to-day is to use it of the completed work of reconciliation between man and God, but the traditional use was to understand by it the means or process by which it was believed the reconciliation was accomplished, namely, the death of Christ. It may be necessary from time to time to make clear the precise way in which the term is being used.

In the meantime we can notice that in the New Testament there is no one cut-and-dried theory of the Atonement. Adams Brown in the *Encyclopedia of Religion and Ethics* distinguishes no fewer than five views to which expression is given by different writers in the New Testament.

The simplest is that which merely connects the suffering of the Christ with his subsequent glory as part of the pre-determined scheme of God (Luke 24.25f; Acts 3.18ff) without offering any explanation.

The second sees a parallel between the death of Christ and a covenant sacrifice. This is suggested by our Lord's own words at the last supper: "This is my blood of the covenant

which is shed for many for the remission of sins." (Matt. 26.28;
Mark. 14.24; Luke 22.20.)

The third makes the death of Christ a ransom or purchase-price by which his people are bought out of their bondage to
sin (Mark 10.45; Matt. 20.28). This also originates with Jesus
himself.

The fourth is the suggestion that in his suffering and death
Jesus bore the punishment justly due for man's sin and thereby
made himself an expiatory sacrifice. This is associated with
the image of the Suffering Servant given in Isa. 53, and through
it links up with the whole sacrificial system of the Old
Testament. As we have seen, this teaching is to be found in
St Paul (Rom. 3.25f; 5.10).

Fifthly, however, there is another view to be found in
St Paul, namely that through the unity of Christ with those
who believe in him they have been caught up into his death
and rising again. They share his experience with him and are
thus made at one with the Father (Rom. 6.3ff).

In view of these varied attitudes adopted by the writers of
our foundation documents one can hardly be surprised if the
teaching of the Church, or of theologians within the Church,
has been flexible and varied. There is a richness about the
teaching on the Atonement that is not exceeded in the case of
any other of the great Christian doctrines. One feels that here,
either by deliberate intention or by the overruling of divine
providence, one has been given great space in which to
breathe and to move freely. As we shall see, there are lengths
to which anyone who wishes to regard himself as within the
main stream of historic Christianity cannot permit himself
to go. But the absence of defined dogma leaves the limits very
wide and makes possible a large liberty of speculation.

This liberty is the first point we must have in mind as we
come to inquire into the doctrine of the Atonement. It will
prepare us for the almost bewildering variety of ideas on the
subject and it will prevent possible disappointment at not
finding ourselves presented with one definite, official, clear-cut explanation. It will perhaps also prepare us to find that

these various ideas are not necessarily opposed to each other. There may be extremes which may be mutually contradictory, but in general they tend to merge into each other. It is therefore possible to hope that one may get the truest conception by trying to hold a number of them together and refusing to be cribbed, cabined, and confined within any one of them exclusively.

The second point to be remembered is that all agree as to the essential fact of a reconciliation or atonement. Man and God were estranged. There was a barrier between them. And somehow for those who accept Christ that barrier has been broken down. In other words among Christian teachers there appears to be no doubt as to the need for an atonement.

This view is not always accepted outside the Church. There are those, for instance, who find in it something rather revolting. In spite of the long history of sacrifice they react violently against any suggestion that God needs to be propitiated. God is our Father, always kind, always ready to receive the sinner. All we have to do then is to turn to him and his arms will be about us. The touching picture in the well-known parable of the father waiting for the prodigal son's return and refusing to listen to any faltering words of apology but ordering his instant glad reception—that is the picture they would for ever hold of God. What need then of any mediator or act of reconciliation?

It is the attempt to answer that question which will occupy a large part of our attention in the following pages. In the meantime we need only remember that merely to ignore faults is not the surest way to remedy them. Nor, it seems, would the deepest instinct of the human soul be satisfied if they were simply ignored. It may be our innate sense of justice or something even more profoundly atavistic, but whatever it is there is something within the sinner himself that cries aloud for the proper recognition and expiation of his sin.

A third point that we shall be forced to notice is the effect upon successive views of the Atonement exercised by changing social and cultural environment. We are all to some extent creatures of our age, our thought forms are inevitably affected by the society in which we live. We tend to explain every issue in accordance with the dominating interests of our own time. To-day we are inclined to frame our answers to all sorts of questions in the light of the evolutionary and relativist theories that are the main pre-occupation of modern science. Similarly in other ages one may expect to find theories of the Atonement coloured by the moralism of the Jews, the power politics of the Roman Emperors, the feudalism of the Middle Ages, the biblicism of the Protestant Reformation, the sentimentalism of the Victorian period.

It would be absurd to suggest that these views are mutually exclusive. Each generation sees a part of the truth. It goes wrong when it thinks it has got hold of the whole truth and proceeds to condemn every other view but its own. Our conception of the Atonement is likely to prove the more complete and satisfying the more it is able to meet all the manifold needs of the human personality.

In this respect there is one further consideration that should be kept especially in mind by those who think of sin as a series of individual acts and consequently as something comparatively superficial which God can easily ignore, cover up, or wipe away. The fact is that sin goes much deeper than that and enters not only into the very fibre of our own nature but also into that of our environment. If it is true, and there are surely none who will deny it, that man is a sinful creature, then it must be clear that his own imperfection must enter into everything he thinks or says or does. Nothing that he makes, in the sphere of literature, art, mechanical invention, business, legislation, law, to say nothing of religion and worship—*nothing* is free from the taint of his sin. Even his very speech shares in the moral imperfection of his whole culture. It is only when we realize this all-pervading character of sin that we can fully appreciate the need for some penetrating and universal remedy. God cannot lightly heal the hurt of his people. Nothing superficial can eradicate the deep-rooted evil of sin. We shall, therefore, expect our voyage of inquiry to take us into deep waters and we shall be properly suspicious of any explanation that seems especially easy and uncomplicated.

We are agreed then that we are dealing with a jewel having many facets. Before we try to deal with some of them in turn we should understand that, like so many of the jewels mentioned in the New Testament, the Atonement is part of a new order of things. We may draw some elements of an explanation from the past, but it is evident that it is itself very much of the present and future. Jesus came proclaiming that the kingdom of God was at hand. On his last night on earth he announced that he was inaugurating a new covenant to replace the old: "This is the new covenant in my blood." As in the old days Jehovah and his people had been bound together under the sprinkling of a victim's blood, so now by the shedding of his own blood Christ was inaugurating a new relationship between his Father and his friends. All who accepted his friendship entered into an entirely new situation. For them was the reconciliation effected and they were to enjoy the fruits of a new union with God.

That is the situation in which we are still living to-day. It is not that we look forward to being reconciled: we are already reconciled. We have to learn what that means, and live in the enjoyment of it. We must try to understand, and understanding to adore. This gives us an intensely personal interest in the inquiry. We are not dealing with some purely academic question. We hope, of course, that our inquiry may help to justify the ways of God in the eyes of some who have not been able hitherto to accept the commonly received teaching on the Atonement and consequently have not pledged their faith to him. The Christian always has an evangelistic purpose in everything that he does, and desires nothing more than to win others to Christ. If that should be the result of this inquiry we should be grateful in the extreme.

But even if that fails, the discussion still has the further purpose of disclosing perhaps to those already converted something new in the rich treasure of their happy condition.

The consideration of each fresh facet will not only bring out its individual beauty but will also reveal some special response that we may or must make. Privilege involves responsibility. If we are allowed "to see the wondrous things in God's law", we have a corresponding duty to reveal their effect in our everyday life. Each fresh beauty, as it awakes a fresh joy in our hearts, should also arouse in us a fresh desire to be active in the acknowledgement and practical expression of what we have seen.

All knowledge constitutes a certain danger. To know and not to do lays us open to the charge of insincerity in the forum of our conscience. Such insincerity would be a denial of the efficacy of the Atonement in our own case. It would be a downfall from a religion into a mere philosophy. "I will show thee my faith by my works." It is the glorious privilege of the reconciled to show, in full confidence and in the details of everyday life, the power of the God who has delivered them from captivity into the liberty of his own family and household.

2

The Example of Love

THE simplest of all the explanations of the Atonement is that known to the theologians as the Exemplarist Theory. This is the view that we are changed in conformity with the example of Jesus. That example is so beautiful, so overwhelming in its beauty, that it has the power to transform anyone who sincerely considers it and is prepared to yield to it. "We needs must love the highest when we see it", and loving it be changed by it.

The typical illustration of this divine alchemy is the incident of the penitent thief on Calvary. In the midst of his sufferings he had evidently been so moved by the patience and calmness of the Person who hung between him and his blaspheming fellow bandit that he attained some kind of belief in the crucified Messiah and prayed to be taken into his kingdom. The contrast between the two robbers has stirred the imagination of Christians all down the ages, and the change in the penitent thief has always been taken as an indication of what the example of Christ can do.

It may well be asked what that example is, and whence its power is derived. The answer will differ according to one's view of Christ's person. If we take an Arianizing or Nestorian view of Christ we may think of him as the highest representative of humanity living out a perfect human life on the natural level, helped by such grace as is offered to every man.

Such a view, it is believed, brings Christ very close to ourselves and awakes in us precisely those emotions we feel for any heroic figure of our race. This must surely be right, so far as it goes.

That is no doubt why the Exemplarist Theory appeals so strongly to those who take a minimizing view of the person of Christ. Here is humanity at its highest and best, showing at one and the same time the most strongly contrasted human virtues: strength and gentleness, mastery and humility, authority and affection. Granted that the Christian view of virtue is the right one, then it is really impossible to fault him anywhere.

But there, we may think, is the rub. If Jesus is not more than man, we have no guarantee that the standard he sets is that of perfection. But what kind of guarantee do we require? Goodness carries its own credentials, it is self-evident. Everyone admires a good man; we have to deny his goodness before we can begin to hate him. "Why callest thou me good?" asked our Lord of the young lawyer, making him search down into his conscience to see how he could justify what might have been a casual politeness. If we cannot recognize goodness when we see it, we must be in a parlous condition indeed. To take good for evil, darkness for light, and light for darkness means that we have sunk into the lowest condition of human baseness.

Actually, however, we do take Christ for more than man. We believe that he is the Incarnate Word of God, that through his humanity the character of God is manifested in human terms. The Incarnation means that Christ's humanity lends itself so perfectly to the purposes of the divine Word that they are one person.

Of course that does not make the example of Christ any the less human. The principle of the Incarnation is that the Word of God will not distort human nature but will speak only in human tones. God will be revealed only in so far as human nature at its best is able to reveal him. We can think of the Son as reflecting the will, the purpose, the character of his Father. The human nature of Christ yields itself so

13

perfectly to the eternal Word that the Word can express himself as perfectly in Christ as divinity can ever be expressed in humanity. And so we see the glory of God reflected in the face of Jesus Christ.

It follows that the heroism displayed by Christ upon the cross (to mention only one incident in a life which in all its parts was a revelation of God) was not only an example of human fortitude but also a manifestation of divine love. Christians have often taken the Cross as an example of God's wrath and have contrasted it with the love and self-sacrifice of Jesus. But that is a mistake. The wrath against sin is but the reverse side of the love for the sinner. The Cross is the outstanding example of God's love.

How can this be, it is often asked, if God is, as we have been taught, impassible, living in a paradise of perpetual happiness and peace? To answer this question at all plausibly we have to think of different levels in the divine being. A great ocean may suffer storms on its surface which have no effect on its unplumbed depths. So God, where he is in contact with space and time, may suffer emotions which do not trouble the calm profundity of his infinite being.

We are taught that the essence of God's being is love. That is in itself a kind of emotion (though in Christian teaching it may have more to do with the will than with the affections); and we can think of it flowing from all eternity in one glad unimpeded stream. But in Christ it deliberately descends into the vortex of human affairs and there, within the sphere of time and space, it suffers the common human vicissitudes. We are told in the shortest verse of the Bible that "Jesus wept". If he is really one with the Father, this sorrow of loving sympathy must be God's. It is eternal love translated into human terms.

In this respect the value of the Cross of Christ is that it shows us clearly what might otherwise have been left to the chances of inference. The sun's ray is revealed by the myriad motes of dust against which it is refracted. Without the breaking or refraction we should not detect the beam. So the love of God striking athwart our sphere of human cares on

Calvary is shown clearly by its suffering for what it is—a love that is ready to suffer to the uttermost to secure the well-being of the beloved.

It is the exemplarist case that such a love, once seen and understood, must melt the hardest heart, as it did that of the penitent thief, and impel us to respond to God's invitation. Thus it would of itself break down any barrier between God and man. "Greater love hath no man than this, that a man lay down his life for his friend." But if while we were sinners Christ died for us—what then? Must we not be overwhelmed with shame and the desire to make amends?

It may reasonably be thought that this was the way in which Jesus looked upon the meaning of his own death. "I, if I be lifted up, will draw all men unto me", he says in the Fourth Gospel. Scholars are now generally agreed that the reference is to his crucifixion. The picture is that of the erection of the bronze serpent by Moses in the wilderness at a time of plague—a dramatic piece of ancient folk-lore that sticks in the memory. Those who were stricken by the plague but looked up to the serpent were healed. To us it may seem an amazing relic of totemistic superstition. But that is not the point. The point is that those who looked on this figure in acceptance and trust were cured. So Jesus, if he is "lifted up", will draw the gaze of suffering humanity to him and as men yield their faith to him they will be healed.

Thus for the author of the Fourth Gospel the Cross is turned from the symbol of shame into Christ's greatest glory. The fact that there could ever be a dispute as to whether the reference here is to the crucifixion or the ascension shows how great an effect the contemplation of the Cross had upon the early Christian generations. It was precisely because they saw it as the great example of love that they were able to overcome the effect of its shame upon the whole reputation and prestige of the new Way and to use it as the great converting medium that it became. The Cross had two sides: on one was the excruciating torture meted out to the most abandoned of human malefactors, on the other shone the blazing light of eternal love. That which was the most difficult element in the Christian Faith to account for and to justify thus became the most powerful of all incentives in the winning and maintaining of others' allegiance. Men saw in the Cross the supreme example of love and realized the extraordinary force of its appeal. Since it represented what they themselves so much wanted to be, it drew them with the irresistible cords of love: they could not escape its attention.

> O love that will not let me go
> I give myself anew to thee,
> I pay thee back the life I owe
> That in thine ocean's depths its flow
> May richer, fuller be.

Of course it can hardly be imagined that the responsive love of man is of the same calibre as the evocative love of God. The love of God is pitiful, compassionate, stretching down from an immeasurable height to reveal itself through Christ to mortal men. Man's love, which it evokes, is twofold: towards God it is adoring, thankful, anxious to serve; towards men it is sympathetic, helpful, anxious always to obtain for others the best possible. Out of the very depths of its adoring love towards God it tries to follow his example in the service of men. This is the reconciliation between God and men, when both are pursuing the same course and fulfilling the common purpose of love.

It seems to follow that wherever we have an instance of genuine, self-sacrificing love we already have some adumbration of the Atonement. God is love, and therefore all love must at least be in his likeness. Anything which shows the characteristic features of love must bring us in touch with him. Christian writers sometimes show fear of this conclusion. They are especially chary of the sentiment conveyed in the lines:

> The picket frozen on duty,
> The mother starved for her brood,
> Socrates drinking the hemlock
> And Christ upon the rood.

Such a collocation of names reveals the inevitable danger of the exemplarist view. The need to put them together in such company as if they were all equal arises out of the desire to show how much of the essential love displayed upon the cross is to be found in the circumstances of everyday life. That desire in itself is excellent. It only becomes dangerous when it seems to suggest that in the Cross of Christ there was nothing more than this. That is a danger we must avoid.

The exemplarist view could not be completely satisfactory if taken alone. It has a great deal to tell us that is valuable and even necessary, but it is only partial. As it stands it is purely psychological. It is superficial. It deals with the emotions as a spring of conduct. But it does not go deeply into the nature of things, nor into the recesses of man's being. There are whole regions of thought and existence that it leaves untouched. Into some of these we shall have to penetrate in the following chapters.

In the meantime it may be well to ask whether it is really possible to know what was Jesus' own mind on the subject of his death. There are those who think that we have no direct evidence on such a matter, and that such views on the end of his earthly life as are ascribed to him in the Gospel are the invention of the early Church. There are few to-day who would wish to deny that the tradition and interpretation of the early Church has any place in the Gospels. Nevertheless we regard it as certain that the despair of ever finding satisfactory ground for an estimate of our Lord's own judgement of himself is unwarranted and will soon become one of the curiosities of criticism. One has to do a great deal of re-writing, for instance, before one can delete from our early records the tradition that Jesus regarded himself as in some sense the Messiah. That he reinterpreted the notion, leaving out much of what he inherited in the chronicles of his race and putting in much that was in closer keeping with his own character, may be taken for granted. The Gospel record indeed claims as much. When one realizes how awkward in the circumstances of the time any open claim to the title must inevitably have been, we can see plenty of reason why Jesus' replies to the questions on the subject must have sometimes seemed enigmatic (cf. Mark 14.62; Matt. 26.64; Luke 22.69f).

Even if we take it for granted that Jesus saw himself as the Messiah, it will not immediately solve our problem about his attitude to his death. A number of scholars prefer to think that the notion of a suffering Messiah was not proper to Jesus but was the invention of devout minds in the apostolic age. Why his contemporaries should be more likely to reach such a conclusion than Jesus himself does not appear. For ourselves we should be much more ready to see what is distinctive of Christianity springing from the teaching of an undoubtedly original personality such as that of Jesus than from the more mediocre, if still striking, minds of his followers. It is difficult to believe that the whole Christian tradition has gone wrong as to the source of its beliefs.

Starting from such a general position we have no difficulty in making at least three assertions with regard to Jesus' attitude to his own death.

First, he foresaw it and deliberately accepted it. The American theologian John Knox in his recent book on *The Death of Christ* makes great play with his view that it would have shown an extraordinary morbidity on the part of Christ so to have contemplated his end. But why? There can at least be no doubt that Jesus regarded himself as a "man of destiny", whatever that may mean. It is notorious that such men feel themselves as set apart to play an unusual rôle in human affairs. They must often be forced to contemplate the possible end of the course they have undertaken. Jesus, for his part, would have been remarkably stupid if he had not recognized that the road he was following might easily bring him into conflict with the leaders of his own people and with the Roman authorities. He must often have deliberated whether he must follow it to the end or change his course while the opportunity was good. Many scholars think the fundamental decision was already made during the temptation that followed his baptism at the very outset of his public career. In any case, the choice once made must have provided him with some bad moments as he saw the end approaching. We can see nothing psychologically improbable or unnatural in the scene in Gethsemane. Anyone who objects to its authenticity on the ground that it is contrary to Jesus' normal calm acceptance of his fate cannot really have thought out the terrible consequences that were to ensue in the passion and crucifixion.

Secondly, if Jesus foresaw his end and deliberately faced it, he could only have done so if he felt it to be something to which he was called and consecrated. "I come to do thy will, O God" was the keynote of his life. The only story we have in the Gospels of his childhood shows him already concentrating on his Father's business. Whether Dean Matthews is right in thinking that filial consciousness was the essential note of Jesus' character, or whether the John Knox already quoted is right in thinking that a prophetic consciousness is more likely to have been Jesus' leading characteristic, in either case he clearly felt himself under complete obligation to do the will of God. What happened to him was of concern to God; and conversely his own concern was to fulfil God's purpose for him. To that purpose he dedicated himself utterly and was prepared to accept the consequences.

It is not necessary to suppose that he consciously pledged himself from the outset to all the dread details of the future, any more than it is necessary to see anything inconsistent in his natural shrinking when those details rose starkly and imminently before him. There must be a moment of recoil when an exposed nerve is touched. But he must have been fortified by the faith that he was working in line with the divine purpose, and that in facing the torture and death he was serving the cause to which he had committed himself in the beginning. "Thus it becometh us to fulfil all righteousness."

Thirdly, if Jesus thus foresaw his end and if he recognized it as fulfilling God's will, he must have been conscious that in accepting it he was in some way revealing the character of God—not in demanding a sacrifice but in being prepared to sacrifice himself to the uttermost. In all his ministry Jesus had tried to satisfy the need of men. He had given himself in work and teaching, in persuasion and suffering, to heal their frustration and to inspire them with hope. Now that the end is upon him and he can no longer escape condemnation, torture, and death, he accepts them as a means of showing how much he (in company with the Father) loves them and is prepared to do for them.

That it might have been possible to explain this tragedy as the work of a vengeful and tyrannical deity is all too clear. The very fact that Jesus is depicted as showing no sign of rebellion shows how fully he had understood and accepted the rôle he was called upon to play. To give, and hold nothing back, is the sign of the greatest love. The agony in Gethsemane and the final prayer, "Thy will, not mine, be done", shows how much submission cost in mental and physical effort; but that it was complete is shown by every detail of the subsequent drama. Having loved his own, he loved them to the end. It can hardly be supposed that in doing so he was not conscious of following divine precept. How else could he have supported the long-drawn-out torture of the preceding days?

It is important to notice that in the long run some such explanation is demanded by the human element in the story. It is not necessary to suppose that such an interpretation requires on the part of Jesus divine foreknowledge of the rôle he was to play. It is true that in the Fourth Gospel John the Baptist is depicted as recognizing at the baptism before ever the ministry began "the Lamb that taketh away the sins of the world". But that may be due to the author's habit of seeing the end in the beginning. In any case such prescience need not have characterized Christ himself. It seems more likely that the full consequences of the rôle to which he quite deliberately committed himself only disclosed themselves gradually to his consciousness. The Incarnation did not involve violence to the human psychology of Jesus. The eternal Word used human nature through which to reveal the Father. If he had wrested that nature from its true condition and made it perform deeds of which human nature even at its best is not properly capable, he would have betrayed the terms of his mission. His would then have been no true Incarnation.

We are, therefore, encouraged to seek an understanding of the development of Jesus' work and witness in human terms, while recognizing that it was precisely through such terms that God willed to reveal himself.

This is the most satisfactory defence and explanation of the moral or exemplarist view of the Atonement. It is of immense value so far as it goes. That it does not go far enough the subsequent pages will suggest. But that is no reason why we should not acknowledge its value as it stands. If we can accept this point of view, it does help us to understand that it is impossible to drive a wedge between Jesus and God. What Jesus did and suffered on the cross was in a true sense a revelation not only of his own character but of the Father.

In the history of doctrine the exemplarist view is associated with Abelard, the great independent French thinker of the twelfth century. In recent times it has been associated with the name of Hastings Rashdall, the English liberal theologian. In both instances it has aroused somewhat violent opposition from orthodox teachers who have thought that it did not allow sufficiently for the legal and traditional views. At the moment, however, the greater opposition comes from the liberal side since it is thought that it presupposes too precise an understanding on the part of Jesus of a relationship between himself and God, which was only made clear in reality somewhat later by the Fathers of the early Church.

It is sometimes said that even the early Fathers thought that the Cross, in so far as it revealed the love of God, showed the result rather than the purpose of God's plan. But in speaking of God's manner of dealing with his universe it is hazardous in the extreme to distinguish between result and purpose. Would anyone say that the revelation of love was not within God's purpose, or that God did not foresee from all eternity its issue on the Cross?

At any rate there can be no doubt at all that the New Testament connects most closely the death of Christ and the revelation of God's love. "Christ died for us while we were yet sinners, and that is God's own proof of his love towards us." (Rom. 5.8, N.E.B.) "God so loved the world that he

21

gave his only begotten Son." (John 3.16.) "It is by this that we know what love is: that Christ laid down his life for us." (1 John 3.16, N.E.B.) "God is love; and his love was disclosed to us in this, that he sent his only Son into the world to bring us life." (1 John 4.9, N.E.B.) Such texts are surely sufficient to lay a firm foundation for the exemplarist view. God so loved the world—that love was revealed in the self-sacrificing death of his Son. When we see it for what it is, we must accept it and respond. As we yield to its influence and strive to follow its example the barriers between God and ourselves are destroyed. Atonement is made and we are reconciled.

3

The Concept of Victory

SINCE we are taking the various views of the Atonement in the order of their simplicity it would seem natural after discussing the exemplarist view to go on to that which regards the death of Christ as the great illustration of his victory.

In 1931 there appeared an English translation of a small but important book by the Swedish theologian Gustaf Aulén called *Christus Victor*. It had for its aim the purpose of bringing back to public notice this view of the Atonement as a universal victory over evil, which, it alleged, was the classic view. For the time being, it asserted, this view had been forgotten. But from the beginning in New Testament times all through the great ages of the Christian Faith the emphasis had always been laid on the victory won by the death of Christ. It is true that quite early there had begun to appear objective interpretations of the death as a kind of transaction, views that had come definitely to the front in the teaching of Anselm. And in modern times subjective views, relying on sentiment (such as the one we have just considered) have become popular. But the classic view, the book asserts, was always that of a great victory.

We may later have to consider how far this judgement is in fact correct. But in the meantime we ought to discuss in what respects the victory was achieved. What is the context of his triumph? Actually there are four contestants over whom Jesus is believed to have shown his power: the world, Satan, death, and sin.

The world is the opponent whom in the New Testament Jesus is said most definitely to have overcome: "Be of good cheer; I have overcome the world" (John 16.33); "Woe unto the world because of offences" (Matt. 18.7); "Jesus Christ, by whom the world is crucified unto me, and I unto the world" (Gal. 6.14); "This is the victory that overcometh the world, even our faith" (1 John 5.4), where "faith" is obviously belief in the Incarnation. In that victory we are given a share: "Whatsoever is born of God overcomes the world" (ibid.); "Thanks be to God, which giveth us the victory through our Lord Jesus Christ" (1 Cor. 15.57).

If it is asked what is meant by the world in this connection, perhaps the most concise answer would be "human society organized apart from God". "The world lieth in the evil one" (1 John 5.19, R.V.). It is this godless society that Christ has overcome by his death. He has ransomed it, bought it back, at the price of his life. Henceforth it is his possession and he can claim it legitimately as his own. It is his by right of conquest. He is the "stronger man" who has conquered the baron's castle, bound him, confiscated his armour, and despoiled him of his goods.

Together with the world Jesus has conquered the Prince of this world. The extent to which the New Testament is committed to a recognition of the importance of the devil and his angels, is very much a rediscovery of modern scholarship. After a period in which we have learned largely to dispense with the personal powers of evil and even to doubt their existence, we have been suddenly jerked back into a realization of the great part they played in the thought of the first century. St Mark's Gospel is seen to be particularly taken up with a description of Christ's long-drawn-out war with the demons.

The first stage of the contest was the temptation in the wilderness. The engagement Christ there won was decisive. Its potentiality was later worked out in many contests with individual demons or with companies of them, in freeing the possessed and in healing the sick. At a moment of exaltation, when certain Greeks had asked to interview him, Jesus saw Satan fall like lightning out of heaven. At another he recognized that even the manner of his death would be a sign of his final victory: "I, if I be lifted up, will draw all men unto me."

Whether in the last resort the powers of evil are proved to be personal or impersonal (and we cannot pursue the question here), the practical position appears to be the same. There can be no doubt that the New Testament as a whole sees the universe as a battleground where the contest between good and evil is fought out. The forces of good are headed by Christ, who could, if he wished, call upon legions of angels to assist him, but prefers to fight alone, using no greater capacity than is proper to man, and relying only upon his Father. Even in the dread moment on the cross, when he felt himself deserted, he did not fail in his steadfast devotion to the good. The powers of evil were unable to break his resolution. The cry, "It is finished", is a shout of victory, and the sense of triumph is further displayed in the peaceful resignation of his life into the hands of God when the victory has been achieved: "Father, into thy hands I commend my spirit."

Appropriately at this moment we remember that the third element in Christ's victory is the defeat of death. In the New Testament death is regularly regarded as the ally and instrument of Satan. Death has three phases: the first is separation of soul from body, which is temporal death; the second is the separation of both soul and body from God, which is spiritual death; and the third is the ultimate punishment of the wicked in their total personality, which is the second or final death.

Christ won the victory over death in all three senses. To us they may seem so distinct that confusion would hardly be possible. In the New Testament, however, the three meanings run into each other in such a way that it is sometimes not easy to tell at first glance which is actually intended. In the early

Fathers physical death appears to achieve priority of consideration. That may be simply because death in that sense appeared much nearer to the general run of mankind than it does to-day. The expectation of life was shorter, the incidence of disease greater, medical attention less scientific, the inhumanity of man to man more general. The contemporary "failure of nerve", about which we used to hear so much, may have meant a seasonal addition to a tendency already there, but it is certain that men at that time found it less easy to escape the thought of death than we do to-day.

Evidence of this state of mind can be seen by contrast with the exaltation of spirit expressed in the exciting pictures of the harrowing of hell, which had their origin in the thought of this period but achieved extravagant elaboration in the later Middle Ages. It can be seen also in the emphasis upon immortality as one of the greatest fruits of the Christian life. Indeed it helped to give a characteristic twist to the eastern view of salvation as a kind of divine alchemy by which mortal nature was transmuted into that which is immortal through participation in the sacraments. It was Ignatius who spoke of the Eucharist as "the medicine of immortality, the antidote against the poison of death". But the sentiment was universal in the east and spread to the west, where it can be found even in St Augustine. Earlier, when baptism still occupied greater attention even than the Eucharist, the same efficacy was attributed to the first sacrament by no less an authority than St Paul: "We were buried therefore with him by baptism into death, so that as Christ was raised from the dead by the glory of the Father, we too might walk in newness of life" (Rom. 6.4, R.S.V.), or as I have ventured to translate it in my *New Testament Letters*: "Isn't that the meaning of Baptism? When we were baptized we shared in the death of Christ. When the water flowed over us it was as if we were in the grave with him. But as Christ was raised from the dead by the power of the Father's glory, so we rise from the watery grave and move freely in a new life."

The victory over physical death stands out all the more clearly for the knowledge that Jesus was not the only competitor in this field. If only one section of the Jews was seriously interested in the question of immortality, it seems that a large proportion of the pagan world was absorbed in it. While the philosophers debated it and sought grounds for its plausibility, the followers of the mystery cults practised rites which they believed would release them from the dread pressure of fate and unite them with a god who would make them immortal. Gibbon pointed out long ago that one of the reasons for the spread of Christianity was the promise it gave of a happy future beyond the grave. If that is so, and there is no reason to doubt it, then it means that elements of the pagan world, having weighed the pros and cons, must have come to the conclusion that Christ's claim to bestow immortality was better founded than that of other contemporary claimants. In other words, those who accepted him must have endorsed the claim made on his behalf that he had won the final victory over death, at least in its physical aspect.

That brings us to the second interpretation of death as separation from God, that is spiritual death, or sin. This, of course, is the very head and fount of New Testament teaching. It was the explanation that was given of the name Jesus ("Jehovah saves"), "he shall save his people from their sins". The consciousness of sin was highly developed among the Jewish people: they are generally recognized as having had a more strongly pronounced moral sense than was common in the first century. Under the guidance of their great teachers they were taught to believe that wrongdoing was an offence against God, that it was, therefore, "sin" in the technical sense. We read a good deal more about sin as moral offence in the Jewish Scriptures than in the literature of other peoples. It is commonly said that if the Greeks were distinguished by their love of art, and the Romans by their skill in law, the Hebrews were distinguished by their highly developed feeling for morality.

Jesus came to deliver his people from their sins. He had to free them from the guilt, the stain, and the power of sin. If sin was an offence against God, it carried with it of necessity a sense of guilt. It was under this sense that the Jewish conscience laboured whenever it was awakened. In the case of a religious genius like St Paul it became an intolerable burden. But in a measure it was shared by all the best elements in the nation. It was one of the main constituents in the Messianic expectation that the deliverer, when he appeared, would set free the nation from the load of guilt incurred through their frequent disobedience of Jehovah. The writers of the New Testament saw that expectation fulfilled in Jesus.

A preliminary warning had been given in the reform movement set on foot by John the Baptist. He had come preaching baptism for the remission of sins. But he had pointed to Jesus as "the Lamb that taketh away the sins of the world". Jesus himself took up the implied challenge as soon as he entered upon his mission. He proclaimed that he had come to give his life a ransom for many. He announced the forgiveness of sins to all who put their trust in him. He used physical healing as a sign of the restoration of spiritual wholeness. In this promise of salvation all well-disposed people could recognize that the kingdom had come, and that the power of sin was already being destroyed.

The triumph could be seen in the Cross itself, normally the symbol of the greatest shame. It was not only round the resurrection that triumphant stories gathered but also around the death of Christ. The portents in the sky, the sudden darkness, the rending of the Temple veil, the opening of the tombs are all expressions of the belief that even in his death Jesus met and defeated the powers of this world which were the personification of evil. Sin in its most dread form, as it held in thrall nature and society, was thus in him destroyed.

This was also true of sin in the sphere of the individual life. It has been pointed out often enough how great an importance Christianity has given to the individual. But the recognition works two ways. If the separate value of each personality has been emphasized and its capacity for greatness made clear, so also has its meanness and its capacity for sinking into the depths of depravity. Jesus taught that the Father set great store by each single person—"The very hairs of your head are all numbered", "Not a sparrow falls to the ground without the

Father's knowledge". Yet each one had his own separate consciousness of need: "Come unto me all ye that travail and are heavy laden, and I will refresh you."

He who cast out the demons from the individual soul, said also to the man sick of the palsy, "Thy sins be forgiven thee". He who told the parable of the prodigal son also called attention to the plight of the single sheep that was lost. He affirmed that there was more joy in heaven over the one individual saved, rescued, or discovered than over all the others put together. Oriental hyperbolism, no doubt; but at least sufficient to show that the victory over sin cannot be complete unless it has been effected in the individual heart and conscience.

The importance of the individual was, as we have seen, a major plank in Christ's platform and was taken for granted in the early Church. St Paul, although he can feel so passionately about the ultimate salvation of his nation, yet makes the faith of the individual the mainspring of his whole system. He taught that through their attachment to Christ believers are rescued from their bondage to the elemental and sinful powers of this world and made heirs with Christ of God. "We also, when we were children, were held in bondage under the rudiments of the world: but when the fullness of the time came, God sent forth his Son, born of a woman, born under the law, that he might redeem them which were under the law" (Gal. 4.3ff, R.V.). Those who have once realized their deliverance from these elemental powers must take the greatest care to refrain from slipping back under their influence again. "If ye died with Christ from the rudiments of the world, why, as though living in the world, do ye subject yourselves to ordinances?" (Col. 2.20, R.V.)

It is clear then that from its earliest years the Church was accustomed to think of Jesus as of one who had come to deliver his people from the world, Satan, death, and sin. It was the figure of the Conqueror that impressed itself on the minds of the early Christians. "Who is this that cometh, with dyed garments from Bozrah, mighty to save?" The demonic picture in Isa. 63 of the conquering Messiah, coming from doing battle with his enemies, his garments dripping with their blood, may have had to pass through the refining influence of Revelation[1] before it was taken up into the literary pattern of Christianity, but it seems to have formed the theme for much of the picture-writing of those early days. Jesus was the conquering hero. Atonement was made with God when upon his cross Jesus destroyed the power of the world, Satan, death, and sin. Salvation is effected for the individual when he places himself under the protection of the Christ and receives the benefit of his atoning work.

Jesus is the conqueror over the death of sin both in society and in the individual. He also proves himself conqueror over death in the final sense of the ultimate fate of the wicked.

It has to be realized that the dawning consciousness of a resurrection did not at first relieve men of their fear of death. Even in the old days death had not meant for the Hebrews total extinction. It had implied a shadowy existence in Sheol, where the ghosts of men lived over again a kind of vague and misty replica of their lives above ground. What had lent its terror to that existence was the belief that during it one was completely cut off from all contact with God (Ps. 88.10ff).

When it began to be felt that existence after death might not bring a deadening but a quickening of sensitivity, the belief was accompanied by a recognition that the new existence beyond the grave would be made appropriate to the kind of life lived by each individual above ground. The author of Daniel asserted roundly that while some would awake to life others would awake to shame and everlasting contempt (12.2). When Jesus had extended the teaching to that of a general resurrection and had endorsed the teaching of a moral judgement on which the future life would depend, it was realized that "the sting of death is sin and the strength of sin is the law" (1 Cor. 15.56). But the Christian could still sing his paean of praise because God had given him the victory through Jesus Christ.

St Paul had complete confidence in Christ as the victorious arbiter of the fate of the world. To quote his own statement

[1] See Rev. 14.20; 19.13, 15.

to the Corinthians: "Then will come the end of the world, when he will hand over the kingdom to God, even the Father, and annihilate every demonic Rule, Authority, and Power. He will have to maintain the rule himself until he has brought all his foes into subjection. The last enemy to be destroyed will be death" (1 Cor. 15.24ff).

What is the relation to this teaching of the "second death" mentioned in Rev. 2.11 is not altogether clear. The phrase "second death" is itself explained in Rev. 21.8 as being the lake burning with fire and brimstone in which extreme and hardened sinners will have their part. Whether that is a symbolic way of foretelling the complete annihilation of all that persists in enmity with God, or whether it is intended to affirm a condition of never-ending torment for the finally condemned, it is not possible to say, although the whole tenor of the Christian revelation would incline us to revolt against the latter conclusion. In any case there can be no doubt that the preceding picture is that of Christ the Conqueror, who has so strongly prevailed against all evil powers that he is able to bring into existence an entirely new creation in which nothing bad can find a place. So much then for the idea of Jesus as victor over the world, Satan, death, and sin.

It is clear that, since Christ was regarded as Conqueror and Christians were "found in him", a necessary element in any adequate picture of the primitive Church will be the notion of triumphant power. We are usually so committed to our contemporary ineffectiveness that we forget that to that original generation the Christian Way did present itself as a movement instinct with power. Extraordinary gifts of healing were expected of those who professed to follow it, thousands were moved by their eloquence, the authorities thought them capable of strong subversive influence, portents were believed to accompany their activities. A victory over the enemies of God in both the material and the psychic spheres was no more than was expected. Christianity had been both in the manger at Bethlehem and on the cross a demonstration, however paradoxical it might seem, of power.

31

This being so it did not seem ludicrous to many members of the Church to compare Christ with Caesar. It would not have been entirely absurd if Pilate really had thought that Jesus professed to be a rival to his imperial master. Augustus, who held the sole power in Rome from 31 B.C. to A.D. 14, had brought peace to the distracted nations. During his reign the *pax Romana* was recognized with gratitude by the civilized world, and he was often given the title of *Salvator mundi*. The very title initiated a rivalry in Christian minds between later emperors and the Christ. The German professor, Ethelbert Stauffer, in his book *Christ and the Caesars* has tried to show how far that rivalry went, even suggesting that some of the more lurid pictures of the Apocalypse are the result of a Christian cartoonist's reflections on the Roman games. Certainly there must have been many who had to choose deliberately between the purple-clad emperor on the throne of the world and the carpenter's Son on the Cross dyed in the purple of his own blood. The mere fact that such a comparison was possible suggests that power, though of a different kind, was a prime constituent of the one picture as of the other. If the one saviour brought peace to the world by force of arms, the other brought rest to the hearts of men by his Cross and precious blood: if the one caught and held the world in thrall by military might, the other won its allegiance by the compulsive power of sacrificial love.

In any case there was nothing weak or feeble about the early followers of the Lord. They had been rescued by a manifestation of mighty power, and power became a leading characteristic of their lives. That was what their neighbours noticed about them.

It was consciousness of his victory in their own case that enabled members of the early generations to possess their souls in patience while their Lord delayed his final coming. At first their confidence in the overwhelming character of his victory was supported by their expectation of his immediate return. He must come in such a manner as to convince the whole world of his superiority. When the years passed and he failed to appear, attention became more concentrated upon his challenge to individuals. We see St Paul wrestling with the problem for the sake of his readers, particularly the Thessalonians. By the time the Fourth Gospel was written the main emphasis had been shifted to the presence here and now of the Holy Spirit. The more intensely one realizes the immediate presence of the Spirit the less real change does one expect at Christ's second coming. Christ cannot very well be *more* present than he is in the power of his Spirit. That is a truth the author of the Fourth Gospel grasped without losing the joyful expectation of seeing him one day face to face. The moment of victory, nevertheless, was shifted from the empyrean into the here and now. Christ is the victor within the arena of our own personality: it will not be a great surprise when we see his victory acknowledged on the battleground of the whole universe.

Thus Christ by his continuous victory effects atonement both for the individual and for the race. It is easy to see how the idea of Christ as Victor could be claimed as the classic key to the interpretation of the Atonement.

4
Substitution

A NOTION closely associated with the idea of the Atonement, and until recently taken for granted, is that of substitution. Christ offered himself, and was accepted, as a substitute for us: he bore the penalty for sin in our place, and we, therefore, escape the proper punishment. That was the general theory which formed the mainstay of generations of evangelical preaching. In our own time, however, it has been subjected to severe criticism both within and outside of the ranks of professed Christians. Yet to many it remains the very essence of the doctrine of the Atonement, far more essential than either the idea of a perfect example, or that of a Christ victorious over the enemies of God and man. We must, therefore, examine it and see how far it can be justified.

At the outset we need have no doubt that the notion is at least adumbrated in the New Testament. Jesus came, according to his own statement, to give his life a ransom for many. It may be doubted whether the phrase strictly interpreted means "on our behalf" or "in our stead". Both forms of expression are actually used in the Greek.[1] But it is improbable that there is really much difference in their application to the present case. It is difficult to see how a life could be successfully given on behalf of others without being a substitute for them, and it cannot have been given as a substitute

[1] Cf. Mark 10.45 with Rom. 5.6.

34

without being given on their behalf. In the sphere of practical relationships the logical distinction disappears. There are many passages in both the Old and the New Testaments that convey the same teaching. We shall have to deal with some of them in due course.

In the meantime we can look at a more fundamental and thorough-going objection to the whole idea of substitution. It is, we are told, illogical, absurd, and unjust that one person should die in place of another. It is true that this sometimes happens in the case of hostages in war. We have the famous example, quoted by Augustine, of the Roman Regulus, who, released by Carthage to negotiate a truce with his people on the understanding that if they did not accept the terms proposed he would return and receive the supreme penalty, first used the opportunity to persuade his countrymen not to accept the terms and then returned and offered himself for death. However, that kind of thing, we are told, does not happen in the proper process of law. There can be no justice in substituting the innocent for the guilty. To give such an explanation of the Atonement is to postulate essential injustice in the very character of God.

We do not wish at the moment to be caught up in any discussion of legal justice—we shall have to consider that subject in a later chapter—but we must point out that as a matter of fact this kind of thing does happen: people do give their lives that others may live. The expectant mother, who learns that she and her child cannot both live and decides to yield her own life in order that the child may be saved, is a case in point. The doctor, who deliberately becomes a "guinea-pig", and dies in providing the information needed for the control of disease, is another.

Instances could be multiplied, but the task is unnecessary, for a moment's reflection is sufficient to satisfy anyone that whether it is contrary to strict justice or not, this is the way the universe is made. People do offer their lives as substitutes for others and the substitution is often effective.

Nor need Christians agree that the principle is necessarily unjust. Of course, if this life were all, then it would be difficult to escape the charge. There is a finality about death that would make it difficult to see what adequate compensation any person who offered himself as such a substitute could ever receive in this life.

But if the present life is not all, if there is an everlasting life beyond the grave, then one can see an opportunity for full and adequate compensation. In the case of such heroism and devotion it is invidious even to seem to bring into consideration the nicely balanced less or more. But we can be sure of so overwhelming a context of joy and satisfaction in the new life that the adequacy of the compensation could never be for a moment in doubt. In any case it is probable that the heroes of such substitution would say that they had received sufficient compensation in the relief they had brought to others.

We may take it then that the idea of substitution is neither foreign to our experience nor alien to common sense. We must, however, be careful to ask in what sense we are applying the term substitution in the present context. In the instances we have just given the substitution achieves its effect on the same level of reality as that on which it was offered. But no one supposes the same to be true of the Atonement. Christ offers his life in order that we may escape death, but not physical death, surely. We all have to die, Christian and pagan alike, "As in Adam all die . . .". What is offered is that we shall not die eternally: "As in Adam all die, even so in Christ shall all be made alive."

The new life in Christ is itself of two kinds: it involves a new moral life here and now, and the permanence of our living personality even beyond physical death. As we saw in the last chapter, Christ gives his life that we may not be overwhelmed by sin, the world, and the devil. He died to make us free. So his death was a substitution on one level in order to win us life on another. He died in the body in order to gain for us life in the spirit. "In that he died he died unto sin once for all, but in that he liveth, he liveth unto God."

It is clear that St Paul is here arguing from analogy, and using physical death as a symbol of spiritual death. Whether he was doing this consciously or unconsciously is doubtful.

Probably the shift in the argument is unconscious. As we have already seen, the term death was itself used ambiguously, and one moves from the thought of physical to that of spiritual death with surprising suddenness. The connection between the physical and the moral seemed much more obvious to St Paul and his contemporaries than it does to us, though they never accepted the identification of the flesh with what was necessarily evil, after the fashion of their Gnostic opponents.

What we have to remember is that although the substitution of Christ did not relieve mankind from the necessity of physical death, it represents a release both from the hitherto accepted consequences of physical death, such as separation from God or complete annihilation, and from the analogous death in the moral sphere.

One of the attitudes of mind that make it difficult for us in our generation to accept such teaching easily is the tremendous emphasis we place upon the individual. We tend indeed to set the individual in a universe of his own and we expect the ends of justice to be completely satisfied in each case separately. No doubt we should all be working towards that end. We recoil at the High Priest's cold-blooded assertion: "It is expedient that one man should die for the people." And we are shocked by what we deem to be the Communist habit of sacrificing the interests of the individual to those of the mass, as we may suppose is the custom of bees and ants. We may even resent the indifference of nature herself, "so careful of the type she seems, so careless of the single life". Perhaps we need, at any rate within the terms of this present life, to strike some sort of balance between the claims of the individual and those of the community.

Certainly if we go back to the Old Testament we shall find an implicit acceptance of the solidarity of the race that is far removed from our way of thinking. As we have already seen, it was the family rather than the single member that was the unit of society, and this recognition of a multiple unity at the heart of society made it easier to recognize a tribe or a whole people as having a unity of its own. Everyone is familiar

37

with the way in which a culprit could be discovered by the use of the sacred lot, at each stage narrowing down the search and successively eliminating all but one tribe, one family, and at last one individual. It is even more significant that when finally Achan has been thus convicted of looting he does not suffer alone but all his family suffer with him. Similarly in the case of the rebellion of Nadab and Abihu all their families are overwhelmed in the catastrophe that overtakes the leaders.

To us this may seem desperately unjust, but it would not appear so to a generation that had scarcely begun to think in terms of the individual. It seemed to them a law of nature that if one member suffers all the members suffer with it. But it followed too that if one member had a great access of good fortune, all the family should enjoy it with him. This solidarity of the family made it seem natural that one member should offer himself on behalf of the whole. The old habit of offering the first-born, and the later habit of offering some kind of substitute for him, consecrated the whole family.

When Jeremiah and Ezekiel begin to set the emphasis on individual responsibility it is obviously so strange and unexpected a teaching that they have to spell it out in words of one syllable for their people. The soul that sinneth it shall die. The people who eat the sour grapes shall find their own teeth on edge, not some future generation. The really important law is not that which was engraved on tables of stone but that which is written in the heart of each believer.

So at last the individual begins to come into his own. But his importance is not intended for his own glorification. The claims of the community are still strong. It is not long before we find an individual pictured as offering himself not for another individual only but for his whole people. The Servant Songs of Isaiah, particularly chapter 53, are the finest examples in literature of the recognition of vicarious suffering.

The principle remains the same even if we accept the exegesis of some scholars and regard the Suffering Servant as a personification of the people of Israel as a whole or of a saintly nucleus within the nation. The personification suggests the essential unity and the suffering affirms the substitution: "For the transgression of my people was he smitten;" "Surely he hath borne our griefs and carried our sorrows"; "He was wounded for our transgressions, he was bruised for our iniquities: the chastisement of our peace was upon him; and with his stripes we are healed"; "The Lord hath laid on him the iniquity of us all"; "He shall bear their iniquities. Therefore will I divide him a portion with the great, and he shall divide the spoil with the strong; because he hath poured out his soul unto death: and he was numbered with the transgressors; and he bore the sin of many, and made intercession for the transgressors."

These familiar phrases from the fifty-third chapter of Isaiah affirm the principle of substitution more clearly than any other passage in the Old Testament. Nevertheless the idea was made familiar to the Israelites by other elements in their national life and customs. We leave on one side the identification of the King with his people, and his substitution for them in certain elements of their ritual, as being highly debatable ground. Nor will we stop to consider the significance of the names of the twelve tribes on the breastplate of the High Priest. Nor need we enter here into the whole question of sacrifice, which will engage our attention later. But we must refer to one element of the Day of Atonement, which seems exactly to the point. This is the ceremony associated with the scapegoat.

Upon this goat, it will be remembered, hands were laid in token of the transference to it of Israel's sins and it was then sent out into the wilderness to Azazel, the spirit of the wild. Here it seems the goat is deliberately made a substitute for the people: it endures the fate that might have overwhelmed the whole nation. It is small wonder that so vivid a piece of symbolism sunk so deeply into the consciousness of the early Christians, and presented itself to them as a picture of the Christ. The wonder is that it does not seem to have caught the imagination of contemporary Jews and taught many others, like the author of the Servant Songs, to find in it a picturesque assertion of the religious principle of substitution. Perhaps it was the rising insistence on the seemingly contrary principle of individualism that diverted attention from the truth it contained.

The reconciliation of the two opposed principles had to await the advent of the New Testament period. There the emphasis on the importance of the individual is shown as part of Jesus' characteristic teaching: "The very hairs of your head are all numbered"; "Are not five sparrows sold for two farthings? Yet not even the one thrown in for luck can fall to the ground without the Father's knowledge." At the same time there is a collateral emphasis on collectivity: "Fear not little flock, it is your Father's good pleasure to give you the Kingdom"; "Where two or three are gathered together in my name"; "That they all may be one; I in them and thou in me." Jesus' continual stressing of the community in such parables or analogies as that of the vine and the branches reinforces the lesson.

The normal reader of the Bible can hardly doubt that the idea of uniting the two principles together and regarding himself as in some sense a substitute for his whole people as for each individual was in Jesus' own mind.

The mind of the modern expert on New Testament criticism, however, is not so clear on the subject. In the course of his studies he has been forced to ask himself how far the idea was that of Jesus himself and how far it was put into his mouth by such early followers as were responsible for the formation of the apostolic tradition. Did Jesus really think of himself as Messiah at all? Did he go on to apply to himself the notion of a suffering Messiah as adumbrated in Isa. 53? These are grave questions and demand a considered answer. Here it can only be said in quite summary fashion that criticism appears at the moment to be passing through an over-anxious and meticulous phase. It is doubtful whether some of the questions it is asking can ever be answered with scientific accuracy. Many of the answers given must, therefore, be largely subjective. They reflect the mind of the twentieth century rather than that of the first.

That it was by no means unknown for demagogues or insurrectionaries to give themselves out to be the Messiah is a commonplace of the period. It would have been very odd if at least some of Jesus' contemporaries had not taken him for Messiah, and if he had not been forced to reflect upon the point himself. And if he had so reflected, what more likely than that he should see himself as an unusual kind of Messiah, one who would conform to the picture of the Suffering Servant rather than, shall we say, to that of David Redivivus? If, as apparently no one would doubt, the coming of the Messianic kingdom was a subject of Christ's teaching, could the notion of a Messiah be so very far behind?

Granted then that Jesus was compelled to think of himself in connection with the Messiahship, it seems at least likely that he must have been led to reflect upon the connection of that mystical figure with the Suffering Servant painted by the prophet. It is indeed possible that he was the first teacher in Israel to see, or at least to make much of, that connection. He had at least as much perspicacity as his followers, and they were not slow to pick up the idea. So St Peter in the first epistle bearing his name describes Jesus as one "Who his own self bore our sins in his own body on the tree, that we being dead to sins, should live unto righteousness; by whose stripes ye were healed" (2.24); and again "Christ also hath once suffered for sins, the just for the unjust, that he might bring us to God" (3.18).

If the principle of substitution is to be accepted at all, it would seem that it would be altogether appropriate that the substitute for us should be one of ourselves. It would be more in line with the fitness of things than that he should be either an angel or a scapegoat. And that for two reasons: only one who shares our human nature would have the adequate sympathy with us in heart and mind and experience, and also he would fit most completely into the actual circumstances of those on whose behalf he suffered.

To take the latter point first. As we saw in the last chapter the whole of our human situation has been vitiated by sin. The consequences of sin have extended to our entire social environment. That environment needs, therefore, to be redeemed in its totality. The most appropriate substitute for it is one who himself belongs to it and yet, since he has not himself sinned, would not need to suffer on his own account. Such a substitute could only be found in Jesus, the sinless Son of Man. He was, in St Paul's dreadful phrase, "made sin" on our behalf (2 Cor. 5.21). Though he had committed no fault, he accepted for us the severest penalties of sin.

The earlier point should be even more clear. It was fitting that one who offered himself as a substitute for us should at least know by actual experience what it was all about. It is true that, not having sinned, he could not know the dejection and misery of his own sin. Yet out of the intensity of his sympathy and his association with every kind of human failure he must have had sufficient experience of "the weariness, the fever, and the fret, here where men sit and hear each other groan". Jesus was not a person who could not be touched with the feeling of our infirmities, but was one who was tempted as we are, yet without sin. As the only person of that calibre who has ever existed, he was the only possible substitute.

There is a story of a Philippino chief who had been trying to wean his people from their more barbarous practices, especially that of human sacrifice, and seemed to be succeeding. There came, however, a time of intense drought followed by severe famine. The people were convinced that the anger of the gods would be appeased only by a reversion to the old manner of sacrifice. Having tried in vain to hold them back the chief gave way and said they should have their victim. When on the stated morning they came to collect the person destined to be offered and the cloth was removed from his head he was seen to be no other than the chief himself. Needless to say the device of human sacrifice for such a purpose was never resorted to again.

Who is to say that such a substitution was not efficacious? It may not have been logical: it certainly falls into no legal category. But in discussing the Atonement we are not really dealing with logical or legal categories. As we often have

42

occasion to see, matters of religion are best dealt with on the personal level. Reconciliation between persons is generally effected outside the sphere of legal and logical considerations.

Those who have lived through two world wars have good reason to recognize this truth. When we speak of other people having died that we may live, we are not giving utterance to idle platitudes. We do know that but for the self-sacrifice of those others we might not be alive at all to-day, much less living in peace and freedom. Substitution is not a theological formula or a vain fantasy. It is a fact of everyday life—as every parent knows. "Would God that I had died for thee, O Absalom, my son, my son", David cried in vain.

Here in Jesus Christ is one who did die for us. The privileges we now enjoy with God we recognize as the fruits of that death. It is still true that we have to die, but we need not die eternally. Being reconciled with God we enjoy the new life in him both now and for ever. And this we do because Jesus poured out his soul unto death on our behalf.

5

Transaction

WE have now examined three facets of our jewel. We have thought of the Atonement as the work of Christ under the aspects of example, victory, and substitution, and we have dwelt upon the essentially personal qualities involved in these points of view. Many, however, of the great historical attempts made to interpret the Atonement have used less personal categories of thought. All the same, as they have meant a great deal to past generations of Christians, we should make a mistake if we did not ask whether they still held some meaning for us. In this and the next chapter we shall be thinking of explanations of this less personal type.

In the present chapter we think quite baldly of the Atonement as a transaction. It may seem almost revolting to use such a term in such a connection. But on reflection it may not seem quite so repulsive as it at first sounds. There are after all such things as principles, eternal standards of right and wrong, absolute qualities of justice and truth. It is contrary to our notion of the fitness of things that these principles should be ignored or betrayed. Especially in our dealings with God, who *ex hypothesi* is himself the very embodiment of every good and perfect gift, is it necessary that such standards should be fully acknowledged. Whatever theory we adopt to explain the means of our reconciliation with God, it must justify itself, not only on the level of our human behaviour but also, so far as we can judge, in the most exalted sphere of absolute standards.

As the ages progress and sophistication grows, we become more apt to isolate ethical principles and to treat them almost as if they were elements in mathematics. It is the inevitable result of the effort to generalize or universalize. That indeed has always been the tendency in philosophy. Such subjects are easier to deal with in argument when they have become mere symbolic counters in the game of thought.

It is true that at the moment there is a rather violent reaction going on among philosophers against this species of abstraction and depersonalization, and to that extent we are being taken back (unintentionally) to the Old Testament manner of thinking. The Hebrews were never philosophers in the classical sense of the term. They were never at ease with abstract considerations: they always thought in terms of the personal and concrete. Even notions like wisdom, truth, law, they had to personalize before they could deal with them happily.

Perhaps it was this habit of thought that helped to give them their acute sense of sin. Wrongdoing was not just failure, frustration, or feebleness: it was offence against God. That is what made it so serious. Even unintentional wrongdoing was sin and must be atoned for, while it was doubtful whether intentional and deliberate sin could be atoned for at all.

The need to keep the nation righteous was paramount in the mind of priest and prophet alike. The latter enunciated the principles, and the former framed the laws by which the principles could be exemplified in daily life. In both cases the standard was represented by the will of Jehovah. It was not a question of trying to attain an ideal, but simply of doing his will as thus expounded. As mankind had continued to do wrong since the first sin of Adam and Eve, it followed that there was a grave accumulation of debt to be paid off as well as a continually running debit account to be met.

Accommodation could only be made by sacrifice, which is a gift given to God to square accounts. Hence the long-drawn-out training of the Hebrew people in a sacrificial system which grew more complicated with each successive revision. Whether the law was ever actually put into practice in its most elaborate formulation may be doubted, but at any rate there was sufficient of it in current use to keep always before the mind of the faithful Jew the horror of sin and the difficulty of making amends. St Paul's early career, his determination to get right with God and subsequent anguish were the logical outcome of the system.

What was behind this sacrificial cult, this idea of making presents to God in order to circumvent the effects of sin? There seem to have been two fundamental thoughts: the first that if a man has committed a wrong he must make amends—that is the principle of expiation; the second that if God has been offended he needs to be brought again to look kindly upon his worshipper—that is the principle of propitiation. Both principles are at work in the Old Testament system of sacrifice and they are largely responsible for the view of the Atonement as a transaction, that is, an arrangement by which man can purge himself of his sin and appease the anger of God. We must examine both principles a little more closely.

The idea of expiation no doubt starts from the need to repay what one has wrongly taken. If exact repayment is not possible, the nearest equivalent must be sought. It is the *lex talionis*, the law of retaliation. It ensures that the culprit shall pay up, and at the same time protects him against any demand for excessive or unjust payment. It begins with the exaction of an exact replica—an eye for an eye and a tooth for a tooth; but it becomes progressively more humane and soon allows for the payment of a substitute equivalent. Thus animal sacrifice is substituted for human sacrifice, a change which is thought to be adumbrated in the incident of Abraham and Isaac and the ram caught in the thicket.

The idea of expiation, which is well recognized in the law of all countries, thus followed the same general line of the modification of the blood feud among our own Anglo-Saxon ancestors. Where originally the family of the man slain could demand the death either of the slayer himself or of some member of the slayer's family in compensation, later it was agreed that some other payment could be made, according to the rank of the person slain; and that payment was held to expiate the wrong and end the feud. Similarly the sacrifices of the Hebrews were nicely apportioned to the sin committed and were believed to expiate the crime.

But what penalty could be adequate to expiate the sin of man? His age-long rebellion against God, shown up in most lurid light by his rejection of Jesus, was a sin that would admit of no ordinary effort at payment. For the utmost sin the utmost penalty must be demanded. As the victim, goat or lamb, offered in sacrifice had to be "without blemish", so the one who offered himself to expiate the total sin of man must be without sin. That rôle could be filled only by Jesus of Nazareth.

> There was no other good enough
> To pay the price of sin;
> He only could unlock the gate
> Of heaven, and let us in.

Thus by the sacrifice of Christ our sin is expiated—the penalty has been paid. What about us then? Do we escape punishment altogether? Many of the best Christians do not like to think so: they say they could feel much happier if they could bear some of the punishment and share some of the sufferings of Christ. T. E. Lawrence has a story about two of his Arab boys who were the firmest of friends but were always leading each other into mischief. At last one of them overstepped the bounds altogether and had to receive a severe beating. When the second saw how his friend suffered he did not run away but came and asked if he might be punished too, so that they might share the pain together.

Many of us would similarly like to share the sufferings of Christ. We know that we cannot share them to the full, they are beyond our comprehension: "We may not know, we cannot tell what pains he had to bear." In any case the effect of his suffering is precisely to spare us the chief pain of all, separation from God. But we still have to bear the pains to

47

which mankind is naturally heir, and there is bound to be a residuum of suffering even when modern medicine has done its brilliant best for our relief. We can at least then ask Jesus to take this residue of pain and permit it to be used along with his for the relief of suffering humanity.

How far such a sharing can be regarded as a real expiation of sin cannot properly be determined. It is perhaps true that one can never wholly expiate sin. Certainly we can never do it of ourselves even on the human plane. But God's mercy is greater than man's. The only way in which it can be done is to acknowledge our own inability and unite ourselves with the offering of Christ. The more closely we are associated with his perfect sacrifice, the more we shall feel that our accounts are settled with God, and that, now that he has blotted out the "handwriting of offences" that was against us, we may start afresh with new life and hope.

If the idea of expiation is not easy for the modern Christian to assimilate, the idea of propitiation is still more difficult. To propitiate suggests making favourable someone who is not already favourably disposed. To think of God in such a way is not easy for the Christian. We are brought up to picture him as the most loving and fatherly of beings. Further we are taught to think of God as of one who never changes, "with whom is no variableness neither shadow cast by turning". But if he has to be propitiated it seems to mean that he is first angry and then can be induced by some action to become benevolent. This, of course, would be a caricature of the Christian idea of God.

We cannot disguise from ourselves the fact that this idea of God as a God of wrath has sometimes been maintained. It was indeed one of the oldest Christian heresies. As long ago as the second century Marcion, the Gnostic heretic, was so obsessed by the anger attributed to God in the Old Testament that he cut out the whole of those books from the list of sacred writings together with such parts of the incipient New Testament as seemed to him to endorse that idea of God. The same view has frequently cropped up in the course of later history. It was expressed in modern times by the heroine

48

of Olive Schreiner's *Story of a South African Farm*: "I love Jesus but I hate God." And who is there who has not in his more childish moments distinguished between the gentle Jesus and the avenging God?

There is, of course, no justification for such discrimination. We can only see God as revealed in Christ. We must no doubt make allowances for the slow education of the chosen people through Old Testament times. But even there God is most clearly depicted as the father of his people. In the New Testament, as we have already seen, the very purpose of the Incarnation is to make clear the true character of God. And there the culminating statement is, without the slightest doubt, "God is love".

How then can we associate such a God with the need for propitiation? Is God angry at all? The answer must be the old-fashioned one that while God loves the sinner he hates the sin. This may seem satisfactory until we realize how difficult it is to dissociate a man from his actions. How much of our sin originates in our own will? There must, therefore, be some sense in which God's displeasure flows over from the wrong committed to the person who committed it.

We who are wrongdoers cannot help having this in mind when we approach God. Left to ourselves we would hardly dare approach him at all, but in Christ we can still come, with humility certainly but also with boldness, knowing that he has already made propitiation for us. Christ has offered to God the guarantee that in him we have turned our back upon the old life of darkness and our faces to the light. Someone indeed has suggested that when we approach God from the environment of our sins we are looking at him through dark glasses and inevitably see his face without the sunlight of his love shining from it. But when we look at him from within the environment of Christ's love we see him "face to face" without any intervening medium to tone down the brightness of his love, which is indeed the selfsame light as beams from the face of Christ.

The fundamental change, therefore, is not in God but in ourselves. "We love him because he first loved us." God is, and always has been, the very perfection of love. This does not mean indulgence. The more truly we love a person the more we are sensitive to his faults and shortcomings. To perfect love everything is revealed. This need not involve a hyper-critical or censorious attitude. It suggests only the earnest desire for ultimate perfection. That desire should be met by the willing co-operation of the beloved, rendered perhaps almost unconsciously, but sufficiently to allay our anxiety and to establish harmony of relations between us. It is in some such way that God looks upon us. Christ has come forward as a guarantor of our upward desire. God is thus propitiated, and with Christ we freely offer ourselves to him.

We can thus still see some value in the ideas of expiation and propitiation. It is true that they do not come readily to our minds in this generation. They belong more properly to an age when ritual sacrifice was an essential element in wor-ship or when people still lived under the shadow of a law in which the main effort was to make the punishment fit the crime. To-day we pride ourselves on not judging one another and on maintaining the tolerant principle of "live and let live". So we fancy we never need to be propitiated. We also think, or fancy we think, that the only rational element in punishment is the recovery of the sinner. Expia-tion, therefore, is out of date: we do not ask anyone to pay for his wrongdoing, only that he shall not repeat it.

That represents the advanced thought of to-day. There is a great deal in it, but like most "advanced" thought it has probably gone too far. Certainly when people are no longer arguing about public law but are just concerned with their own private concerns, they show plenty of capacity for anger and are ready enough to make their relative or neighbour pay up for any wrong he has done them. We are, therefore, not so far removed as we sometimes imagine from the world of thought in which the old theologians moved when they brought the ideas of propitiation and expiation into their attempt to explain the Atonement. It is possible that as fashions change these ideas may again become common currency. But it is to be hoped that if they are applied to God it will be with the reservations and qualifications we have already suggested.

In the meantime it may help if we look again at the New Testament to see whether there is found any place there for this transactional idea of atonement, and in what sense, if any, it uses the ideas of expiation and propitiation.

That there was some transaction in the sense at least of an ordering of the universe in such a way as to save man while still observing the ends of justice is obviously the view of St Paul. It is actually the central point of his whole philosophy of history. Man was promised salvation on the understanding that he should serve Jehovah. When he failed in that service he was put under the law, which was intended to ensure obedience. When man still proved recalcitrant, Christ, the incarnate Son of God, fulfilled and superseded the law, paid up the demands that it had made, set matters right with God, and offered salvation to all who would join themselves to him by faith.

In this way the divine economy was justified. If the law had failed, it had not gone for nothing. It had preserved the idea of perfection, had made men realize the impossibility of attaining the ideal by their own exertions, and had led them up to Christ who had shown himself the perfect Man. Thus the law, which was a curse to men when they tried to keep it in their own unaided strength, was a blessing to those who by it were brought into touch with Christ. Jesus thus fulfilled the law and brought the era of its dispensation to a conclusion by bearing its full penalty. "Christ hath redeemed us from the curse of the law, being made a curse for us: for it is written, Cursed is everyone that hangeth on a tree" (Gal. 3.13). By thus accepting the condition of a person "accursed" Christ has expiated the sin of all who are prepared to take advantage of his substitution of himself for them.

That he has also in some definite sense propitiated God is revealed by the author of the Epistle to the Hebrews. In the view of that writer no other kind of being but man could represent man to God. That was the purpose of the Incarnation. Not even the angels could do it but only one who,

51

"being the brightness of [God's] glory and the express image of his person, and upholding all things by the word of his power, when he had by himself purged our sins, sat down on the right hand of the Majesty on high" (1.3). This purging of our sins he accomplished by filling the full purpose and intent of the law. When one came to think of it, it was really impossible that the blood of goats and bulls could wash away sins. The only adequate offering must be that of a perfect human life. So in offering himself Christ brought to a perfect conclusion the whole long line of sacrifice. But he was not only victim but priest. He offered himself and so fulfilled the functions of the long line of Jewish priests. Indeed he belonged to a better stock than they because he came of the mystical line of Melchizedek, which was both royal and eternal. So Christ had only to offer the one perfect sacrifice of himself and God was reconciled for ever. "This man, after he had offered one sacrifice for sins for ever, sat down on the right hand of God . . . for by one offering he hath perfected for ever them that are sanctified" (Heb. 10.12, 14).

St John is of the same mind, although he expressed himself under a different metaphor. He thinks in terms of the law courts, and sees the prisoner at the bar relying with utter trust on the barrister who is pleading for him. "If any man sin we have an advocate with the Father, Jesus Christ the righteous: and he is the propitiation for our sins: and not for ours only but also for the sins of the whole world" (1 John 2.1f). In this sentence the significance of the term "propitiation" appears to include that of "expiation", thus exposing the fact that man's expiation of his sin through Christ is the reverse side of his propitiation of God through the same agency.

There is one passage in the account of the passion which has always struck the Christian imagination as the most graphic illustration of the cost of this transaction to Jesus himself. It occurs as the only words that Mark and Matthew record from the cross. It was immediately after the darkness, a physical darkness that corresponded with the near despair of the crucified Saviour: "My God, my God, why didst thou forsake me?" No doubt the cry was a quotation from Ps. 22, a well-known hymn of the Lord's childhood. No doubt too the cry was not uttered until the sense of God's presence had been recovered. Nevertheless it has always been regarded as representing the lowest depth of agony into which any human being ever sank. We have more than once had to refer to the fact that separation from God is the greatest evil from which man can suffer. Yet Jesus had to bear that ultimate pain, and that at the very moment of his most exquisite physical suffering. This was the greatest of all sacrifices, the loss of the sense of his Father's presence. Particularly must this have been excruciating for one whose every moment, as we have pointed out, was lived in dependence on the felt and experienced will of God.

Than this sacrifice could go no further. It means that all that man could do, even perfect Man personalized by the eternal Word of God, had been done. The transaction was fulfilled, the debt had been paid, God and man had been reconciled. Henceforth love could flow free and unhindered between man and his Maker.

To dismiss all this as mere symbolism or picture-writing would be a gross error. No doubt it is truth expressed in human language and the drama may be capable of interpretation in more abstract terms than tradition has employed. Nevertheless the essential truth is there. The demands of justice had to be met. Jesus deliberately sacrificed himself in order to meet them, and of that sacrifice we are the beneficiaries to-day.

6

Satisfaction

In discussing the conception of the Atonement as a kind of transaction, of which the eternal reality is reflected in the historical events of Jesus' passion, we have found ourselves hovering between the abstract and the concrete, between the ideal and the personal. Much the same will be found true of our present consideration, which is a subsidiary notion to that of transaction. Even if we were to abandon the notion of a formal transaction as too naïve or too picturesque, we should still be left with the feeling that any suggestion of a reconciliation between God and man would be gravely deficient if it left unsatisfied the great principles of truth and justice. Nature abhors a vacuum, and there is such a vacuum if no satisfaction is made.

It is this sense of something still lacking, as we shall see in a later chapter, that has led some thinkers to throw doubt upon the whole conception of forgiveness. Evil is evil, it is said, and demands some kind of reparation. Merely to forgive and forget is no solution. If no reparation is made, the ends of justice are defeated and the organization of the universe is left an untidy mess.

We have no wish to anticipate now what will have to be said later on the subject of forgiveness. But it is necessary before we go any further to take up this notion of satisfaction and to see what allowance is made for it in the Christian tradition.

Let us say at once that it appears to be fully recognized in our Lord's own teaching, at least in so far as that is presented to us in the Gospels. No one could possibly be blind to his insistence on the need to establish the right relations with God. That indeed was the keynote struck by his forerunner John the Baptist: "Repent ye for the kingdom of heaven is at hand." And that was the text taken up and constantly reiterated by Jesus.

The very command to "get right with God" implies that some satisfaction has to be made. Jesus did not talk in terms of abstract principles: he was as personal as were all the men of his race in his whole manner of thought. He did not think of truth, beauty, goodness, as abstractions but of persons who embodied those qualities: "I am the truth"; "Solomon in all his glory"; "There is none good but one, that is God." Consequently he does not proclaim the need to preserve the nice balance between apparently conflicting ideals but the need to pay our respective debts to God and Caesar. We must expect, therefore, that where a modern philosopher might discourse upon the universal claims of justice, Jesus will speak of the debt we owe to God the Father of us all.

It is significant that he does not regard himself as being outside the range of the demand for satisfaction. He nowhere, it is true, suggests that he must pay for any wrongdoing of his own. Rather he has come to seek and to save those who were lost; and in this very connection he uses the phrase that most clearly illustrates the need for compensation or satisfaction. He affirms that the Son of Man has come to give his life a *ransom for many*, as a price, that is, to buy them back from captivity or slavery.

This may seem a different picture from the one we have already drawn of the *Christus Victor*, the conquering hero, who by might of arms delivers his people and destroys their enemies. But this is Jesus' own picture of himself which must be put beside the other; a purchaser recognizing that a price has to be paid and offering himself in payment for those who are to be released. It is the concession Jesus makes to the notion of satisfaction. His people are not to be snatched away in defiance of all law but are to be acquired in accordance with the strict claims of justice. The proper price will be paid.

It is perhaps unfortunate but nevertheless inevitable that, once mention is made of a price, the question immediately arises to whom it is to be paid. Jesus had done no more than mention the word "ransom", but, as we have already seen, the whole tenor of his teaching made it clear that the ransom was to be from the world, death, sin, and the power of Satan. For his immediate contemporaries that seems to have been sufficient. But once the tradition had been fixed and recorded, imagination began to play on it and gaps had to be filled. Particularly men began to ask, if Jesus paid a ransom to deliver us, to whom was that ransom paid?

An early answer was, "To the devil". Startling as this may seem to us, it would appear quite natural in the third century, when it was first taught by the great Alexandrian scholar Origen. Men were well accustomed to the payment of ransom in his day: it was one of the common features of social life. A large proportion of mankind were slaves and their numbers were frequently increased by the addition of prisoners taken in war. It became one of the duties of charitable bishops to buy such slaves back and to give them their freedom. Inevitably in such cases the first question to ask was to whom the price should be paid. Naturally then if Jesus gave himself as a ransom for many, one must ask to whom he gave the ransom price.

That the answer should be the devil was also natural enough considering the state of thought at the time. The oriental manner of thinking was, as we have seen, even in the Hellenized cities, strongly personal. People did not think instinctively of a principle of evil but of a personal devil. He was the enemy who held the souls of men in thrall. They had sinned against the light and sold themselves to the devil; from him justice demanded that they should be bought back. It was Jesus who paid the price and thereby retrieved them.

To some this plain statement of the case seemed to be altogether too favourable to the devil. It put him on a sort of trading equality with the Christ and showed too much courtesy to one who was the source and sustainer of all evil. Concentration for a time centred on the price. It was, according to Jesus himself, his life. And of course everyone knew that Jesus had given his life upon the cross. But the whole Christian Faith rested upon the fact that he had received it again. God had raised him from the dead. How did that square with the payment already made?

Gregory of Nyssa in the fourth century propounded an ingenious theory. God was pictured as a kind of celestial fisherman angling for the devil. He threw out a tempting bait, the humanity of the Perfect Man. The devil all too greedily snatched it, quite unaware that within the bait was concealed a hook, the divinity of Christ. On that hook he was caught. He may have had some rights over humanity but none over divinity. In thus seizing the Incarnate Word he had overreached himself. To nobody at that period did this method of trapping the devil seem in the least unworthy of God, nor in the least contrary to justice. The devil might think that he could properly lay claim to the humanity of Jesus as to every son of Adam in spite of his sinless perfection, but he certainly had no claim to the divinity of the Son of God. Therefore it served him right to be caught in the very act of grasping a prize to which he had no true claim.

Such an effort to reduce the Atonement to comprehensible terms may seem altogether too childlike to warrant consideration in the twentieth century, although one can remember it as a very effective part of the Sunday School teaching of one's own childhood. Here it is mentioned not only for its historical interest but also to show how seriously was taken at this period the need for satisfaction. It must indeed have been a strongly recognized need if it required such reasoning to meet it.

A far more highly philosophical attempt to answer the same question was made by Anselm, Archbishop of Canterbury, at the end of the eleventh century. This too was not without some reflection of the social background against which it was produced, although recently attempts have

57

been made to suggest that Anselm's theory was a purely logical deduction with no more reference to its environment than a problem in mathematics. However, Anselm's theory does fit in very well with the pronounced feudalism of his times, indeed much too well to have had no connection with it.

The guiding conception of the age of chivalry was that of honour. Each grade of society had its own honour and could demand satisfaction if it were impugned. At the head of society was the king, who was at once the fountain of honour and also the guardian of the rights of all the rest. Consequently the most careful steps had to be taken to maintain the king's honour, and if it were infringed, the most definite penalties had to be exacted.

This conception was transferred to the courts of heaven. The honour of the King of Kings must be paramount both in heaven and on earth. The fate of the fallen angels was sufficient to show what happened when God's honour was infringed. But men also had rebelled and their treason merited everlasting death. For the utmost sin the utmost penalty must be demanded. There was no greater crime than to impugn the king's honour. Man, therefore, stood utterly condemned. But in man's case a way of escape from the tragedy had been found by God's love. His Son would become incarnate. In the life of perfect Man he would be able to suffer the full penalty for man's disobedience. God's honour would then be fully satisfied and man would be reconciled to God. Such is the argument of Anselm's great book *Cur Deus homo* ("Why God became man").

This represents the idea of satisfaction at its completest and most attractive. The notion of honour preserves the ideal character of the conception and prevents it from becoming too materialistic or naïve. It preserves also a very fine and necessary reverence for the character of God. There is a numinous quality about the teaching which we miss in some of the other forms taken by the doctrine of the Atonement. It is an element that is frequently met with in the Bible. "'My thoughts are not as your thoughts nor my ways as your ways;

for my ways are above your ways and my thoughts above your thoughts', saith the Lord" (Isa. 55.8f). To reverence, respect, and honour God is the necessary foundation of all religion. This interpretation of the idea of satisfaction helps us to realize the enormity of sin and the despite it does to God's position. We are thus helped to realize why so desperate-seeming an expedient as an Incarnation was necessary. God became man in order to vindicate his own honour and restore that of all mankind.

Feudal society, however, did not last, and, since each generation must interpret the truth in its own terms, Anselm's idea of satisfaction suffered an eclipse. In modern times interest in his philosophy has restored it to theological notice again, but now shorn of its purely contemporary trappings.

In the meantime a new conception had come to take the place of the old feudalist emphasis on honour, but one in which the idea of satisfaction was equally prominent. This was the idea of law. During the Middle Ages, as the nations, and classes within the nations, had struggled towards greater freedom, the conception of law as an august power over-shadowing both throne and cottage had gradually become distinct. It is true that at the Renaissance and Reformation the monarch had for a time established an absolute claim. But that was not to endure for long and soon the legislature and the judiciary came into their own. Between them they set up and administered a law that was supreme over all other powers even that of the throne itself. Not that the twin authorities of parliament and law court had created the law: they were merely the agents for selecting it and putting it into force. In fact they believed it was already in existence, established in the heavens. Men simply learned what they could of it from revelation and translated it into the terms of their own generation.

Under this overriding idea of an absolute, heavenly, and eternal justice Grotius in the seventeenth century pictured the background of the Atonement as a kind of celestial law court. God the Father was the judge before whom man was indicted and found guilty. When sentence was pronounced

God's own Son stepped forward and offered to pay the penalty. The offer was accepted and its consequences reached their conclusion in that dread moment on the cross when the Father literally withdrew himself and the Son was left forsaken to "become sin" for us and to bear the terrible consequences of sin in complete isolation. Thus and thus only could justice be satisfied and the end of the law be fulfilled.

Of this attempted solution of our difficulty we can say that it recognizes a real need to satisfy the claims of justice and is valuable for that reason. Nevertheless it places the Father in an unfavourable light, which is quite contrary to the general teaching of scripture. It also revolts our sense of the fineness of personal (not to say family) relations, which while it preserves the deference due to justice nevertheless transcends the merely legal aspects of human association. In any case it is probable that we shall never get at any fully satisfactory explanation of our reconciliation to God by fastening our attention on analogies taken from the law courts. We are not dealing merely with questions of abstract justice nor with the logical demands of absolute law: we are dealing with the relations between a loving father and his wayward sons. It is on that personal basis that a solution must be found.

In considering then this question of a ransom we have seen that if we begin asking to whom it is paid we soon land ourselves in grave difficulties. Gregory's answer, "To the devil", seems to our sophisticated ears to border on the ludicrous. Anselm's answer, "To God", while being much more philosophical, drives a wedge between God and Christ and becomes almost unintelligible to a generation that prides itself on having put an end to all privilege and to which honour in the feudal sense no longer has any clear meaning. Further we have seen that the suggestion of Grotius that the price is paid to the abstract principle of justice, while it also appears to oppose the Son to the Father, suffers from a worse defect in that it depersonalizes the whole process of atonement and turns religion into a mathematical problem.

In such circumstances we must get back to our Lord's own statement and ask what it really meant. "The Son of Man is come to give his life a ransom for many." The whole emphasis is on the price and its object. The life of Christ is the price, and ransom is the purpose of the payment. There is not a word about the person to whom the price is to be paid: that thought is not included in the sentence at all. Jesus is thinking of price and purpose and of nothing more. Of course, there is a sense in which the price is paid to sin, the world, and the devil. They are the three powers from which men are delivered: it is they that cost the Saviour his life, and therefore one might say, if one wished to extend the metaphor, that he gave his life in payment to them. But Christ does not actually say so.

Again one might say that, inasmuch as God is eternal justice and eternal truth, Jesus laid down his life to satisfy both principles, and, therefore, he paid the price to them. There is certainly a truth in the view that Jesus offers himself to the Father. He is the representative man, the second Adam, and he must undo what the first Adam did. So, whereas the first Adam was disobedient, Christ was obedient even unto death. He summed up in himself the long line of sacrifice under the law. He offered himself as the supreme sacrifice to which all the others had pointed, showing himself thus both victor and victim.

All this is true enough but it does not mean that in using the term "ransom" Jesus had in mind any possible recipient of the payment. The implicit reference is to past history and to the deliverance from Egypt when Israel was ransomed from its first great slavery. Thus one can see why there is no consciousness of any individual to whom a ransom price was paid. God then redeemed or bought back his people through the miracle of the Red Sea. In all later references the emphasis is on the deliverance: no one ever implies that a ransom price was paid to anyone, either to God or to the Egyptians. So in the transference of the thought to the Atonement, the emphasis is on the deliverance and the cost, not on the recipient of the price which was paid.

There remain two ways then in which the price paid may be regarded as a "satisfaction", the one objective, the other subjective. The former is best expressed in the phrase from our Lord's lips, "Thus it becometh us to fulfil all righteousness" (Matt. 3.15). Everything must be done decently and in order: nothing fitting must be left out. God's plan of salvation is all of a piece and its unity must be preserved by seeing that all promises and suggestions made under the old dispensation are faithfully carried out in the new. This would be a characteristically Hebrew element in the general notion of justice. With everything thus objectively done to meet the requirements of the law there did succeed in the mind of Christ a sense of completion and fulfilment. "It is finished" was his triumphant cry from the cross. It is the sign that he is conscious of having "done that which thou gavest me to do". He has satisfied the ends of justice and in so doing he has achieved his own fullest satisfaction.

Such a view is not just a play upon words. It means that all God's processes hang together, and that we cannot enjoy the fruits of one so long as another is neglected. The Atonement can only be of importance for us if we are caught up in its embrace and made participants in its action. We have already seen that we may hope to contribute our own sufferings to those which Christ suffers and ask him to use them in his work of redemption. So we can contribute the whole of what we have and what we are, sanctified by Christ, to his work for the world.

We cannot pay the price for the redemption of the world. Our recognition of the majesty of God makes us realize how far out of our reach is anything that would be fully worthy of God. For the infinite despite we have done him only infinite reparation would be sufficient. Such infinite reparation only Christ, who belongs to infinity, can offer. But he also belongs to us: we can cling to the skirts of his manhood and bring our own small mede of reparation and satisfaction knowing that it will be gathered into his and used for the taking away of the sins of the world.

7

Vicarious Penitence

MORE than once in the preceding chapters we have had to ask ourselves whether it is right that one person should be called upon to bear anything in place of another. We have had to answer that, whether it is right or not in the terms of strict and abstract justice, that is the way things happen. It may be true that, within the narrow confines of time as we know it on this earth, it is impossible to find a complete vindication of God's ways with men. But no well-instructed Christian thinks that so limited a horizon as that of mortal life will give a final picture of the divine plan. The inquirer has to do the best he can with such data as he finds on the comparatively small stage of history. But he must leave for eternity the full explication of a plan that was conceived before time began.

In any case, quite apart from any question of justification, we have to ask ourselves in this chapter whether we may not find some fresh light thrown upon the Atonement if we consider the possibility of another kind of vicariousness. Granted that the barrier between God and man is due to man's stubbornness, and that there can be no breaking it down without penitence on man's part, and that man shows little readiness to repent, is it possible to substitute someone else's penitence for his? Can Christ, for instance, who has made himself a sacrifice for sin on man's behalf and has borne death and suffering for him, also be penitent in his stead? Is it possible that we can find a fresh aspect of the great reality of the Atonement in a theory of vicarious penitence?[1]

It would seem that a good point from which to make a start in such consideration would be the first word from the cross as given by St Luke (23.34): "Father forgive them, for they know not what they do." We picture the scene: the military guard at the foot of the cross, playing dice to share out the prisoner's clothes, which were their perquisites; the jeering representatives of the Sanhedrin, watching to see the end of their plot; the little knot of faithful disciples grouped around his mother; and on the outside fringe the curious idlers among the passers-by, who have plenty of time to stand and stare. Over all the eye of the Crucified passes, a wave of pity sweeps over him, and he repeats over and over again: "Father, forgive them, for they know not what they do."

It is a poignant scene; and if we are left to contemplate it in devotion, we cannot help being deeply moved by it. But criticism obtrudes itself even in such moments and we must perforce turn our attention to it. Accepting the saying as genuine, we are asked whether it can have any real meaning. What is the significance of forgiveness? Is it just a word, or does it really effect anything?

If it merely means to forget or ignore, one may doubt whether it has any practical consequence. To ask that something may be forgotten is to ask what is not in anyone's power to grant. Our memories are hardly under our control to that extent. Freud indeed said that we forget what we want to forget; but even he would admit that the desire is not a conscious one, and that if it were, its strength would probably impress the event still more indelibly upon the memory. Happily we do forget many injuries, but that is probably because we have taken them in our stride and not paid much attention to them on the way.

The prayer would seem more pointed if to forgive meant to ignore. It would then be a petition that those for whom it was offered might not receive the punishment that was their

[1] See R. C. Moberly, *Atonement and Personality*.

due. To ignore a wrong is to refuse to visit upon the culprit the proper consequences of his wrongdoing. That again is a common human method of dealing with injuries. Often we ignore them simply because we know that if we stopped to exact a fitting penalty for every wrong we suffered we should never enjoy a minute's peace. But is that a worthy motive to attribute to God? If he is the embodiment of perfect justice, if indeed he is the source of all justice, could we justifiably ask him to take no notice of sin? In short has God a right to ignore wrong?

The best answer to all these questions is that this is not what forgiveness means in Christian circles. It does not mean to forget or to ignore. It does not mean anything negative at all. It means something quite positive, a creative activity. It means reconciliation, restoration, replacement in the lost seat of the family circle, re-integration into society and into the affections of those who have suffered the wrong.

It is clear that this creative action of forgiveness is something much more than is implied in the light-hearted and improbable phrase "forgive and forget". It is clear too that it requires more than one party for its effective completion. It needs the co-operation of the person forgiven as well as the readiness of the person who forgives. As far as its effect is concerned, and apart from its subjective value in moulding the mind of the forgiver, forgiveness without the response of the forgiven remains a mere empty word.

Two things may prevent or hinder such response on the part of the culprit—ignorance and pride. He may simply be unaware that he has committed a wrong. He may be so blinded by ingrained prejudice and inherited tradition or even by mere convention that he may not be able to see the harm he has done or is doing. He may be in the condition in which one quite honestly puts light for darkness and darkness for light. He may in this particular situation be unable to discriminate between right and wrong.

This seems to be the state of mind that Jesus discerned in those for whom he prayed: "They know not what they do." The soldiers were blinded by their devotion to duty, the lawyers and Pharisees by their fanaticism, the sightseers by easily accepted conventions. Jesus prays to the Father of all to take their predicament into account and to pardon and restore them.

The other obstacle to forgiveness on the side of the wrong-doer besides ignorance is his pride. He may simply refuse to recognize the wrong when it is pointed out to him or he may deliberately harden himself against any change of attitude on his own part. It is this stubbornness that is perhaps the greatest of all barriers between God and man. So long as it remains even God's forgiveness cannot begin to work. As sulkiness renders impossible all the finer human relations, so this kind of pride is a direct impediment against the love of God. Love simply cannot work while its influence is thus rejected.

We may say at once that the whole reconciling work of Christ was intended to break down this double barrier of ignorance and pride. The two fundamental aspects of his work are revelation and redemption. All his teaching was intended to reveal the true character of his Father and so to enable men to distinguish with the utmost clarity between right and wrong, between truth and falsehood. All his re-demptive work was intended to dissolve man's hardness of heart and to make him amenable to the love of God. On the manward side at least, the Atonement, properly so called, narrows itself down to this action of Christ on men's souls. It is to put them into a receptive attitude, so that God's love can work upon them. It is to prepare the soil so that the rain that falls from heaven may enter in and cause the seeds of the good life to germinate and grow.

We recognize then the need for a receptive attitude on our part. Can we define it further? Before man can open his heart to the creative love of God he must at least be sorry for the past. He cannot turn his face to the light without turning his back on the darkness. Penitence must precede forgiveness, if it is to have the kind of effect we have sketched. One cannot have the new without discarding the old. But everyone who has looked into his own heart knows how difficult is this state of mind to attain. To apologize, to disown our past, to confess a mistake or an injury, to be really sorry and to acknowledge our fault: that is one of the severest tests of human character and one before which many of us fail.

It is here that the thought of Christ's vicarious penitence may come in to help us. He who knew no sin could feel no sorrow for sin of his own. But what he could not feel for himself he could and did feel for us. He who understood better than anyone else what sin meant, he who could probe to the bottom the nature of sin as rebellion against God, he who was himself suffering the bitterest consequence of sin, he inevitably felt more sorrow for sin than any other human being could ever do. "Was there ever sorrow like unto my sorrow?"

But here we must be careful to distinguish between two possible meanings of the phrase "vicarious penitence". When we say that Christ was sorry for our sins, we mean in the first instance that he was sorry because we have sinned. He looks out upon all the heaped-up misery of mankind, and reflecting that in his original intention God had planned the world to be so fair, how could he be anything but sorry for all the wretchedness that man has brought upon himself?

That is surely clear enough. But in the second instance, and that is the real point of the theory of vicarious penitence, we mean that recognizing the sin that is the source of this misery and knowing himself our representative and realizing our lack of true sorrow, he is sorry in our stead and on our behalf. He experiences penitence in our place. Thus a new meaning is given to such phrases as "he was made sin for us", "he was bruised for our iniquities", "he was numbered with the transgressors, and he bare the sin of many, and made intercession for the transgressors", "the chastisement of our peace was upon him; and with his stripes we are healed".

It must be confessed that to many this notion of penitence for others' guilt seems unnatural and unreal. But Bishop Moberly gives an illustration which places the theory where all such teaching should be tested, namely in the family circle. A mother has been wrestling with her recalcitrant children all day and all she has done has only served to increase their naughtiness and harden their stubbornness. Just when a complete *impasse* has been reached the oldest boy comes in, sees at a glance what has happened, and with a cry of sorrow flings his arms round his mother's neck. Immediately on seeing his grief the younger children realize the enormity of their own conduct and are about their mother's skirts crying to be forgiven.

The story may help to solve two problems for us. It may help us first to understand how God can forgive even before the guilty man has done anything to deserve forgiveness. This is not so illogical or immoral a proceeding as it is some-times made out to be. It is a fact that there is, and generally must be, a certain proleptic element in forgiveness. The mother in the story could not forgive the children so long as they remained stubborn and rebellious but as soon as they showed sign of a change of attitude, before ever they had done any "works meet for repentance", she could enfold them with the arms of her love, because she knew that now they were on the right way. So God forgives sinners, not as a reward for any good they have done, but in anticipation of the fact that they will henceforth travel along the new direction in which they are now headed.

But more important from the point of view of our present discussion is the illustration of the way in which men may be brought to repentance. Our Elder Brother with his cry upon the cross flung himself into the arms of his Father, and we realizing the anguish of soul that he experiences on account of our sins, perceive for the first time the immensity of our fault: we are overcome with grief: we are truly sorry: and God's love pours over us, obliterating all the past and carrying us forward into a new life. Christ's sorrow for us acts as the lever which starts our own penitence and gives us the first impulse that carries us into the arms of God.

It might be maintained by the purist that this is merely an extension of the exemplarist view. As on that view Christ's example moves us to the love of God, so on this view his example moves us to genuine sorrow for our sins. That it should do so is no argument against the value of this aspect of the Atonement. Indeed anything that stirs the grace of God

68

within the sinner and leads him to better living must be in line with the Gospel. But the good Bishop Moberly was surely right in seeing more in his theory than this. If we take seriously Christ's representative character as the second Adam, if we feel that he does in mystic fashion sum up the whole human race in himself, then there must be some special value in his expression of a penitence that should be ours.

If it is objected that no one can really be penitent in another's stead, one is bound to ask whether the objector is not guilty of trying to substitute logic for life. Another domestic episode may illustrate the point. A small girl was discovered weeping while her still smaller brother was being reprimanded for a glaring fault. "But why", she was asked, "are you crying? You didn't do it and no one is vexed with you." "I feel so ashamed for him", was the totally unexpected reply. She was really feeling acutely the shame that he ought to have felt. Was not that an instance of vicarious penitence and had it no value in the sight of God? Certainly it must have had a value in the sight of the brother if he had known of it.

Everything that can release and allow to flow freely the healing waters of forgiveness and reconciliation is of benefit to mankind. It is perhaps our failure to recognize this need in our relations with God that has brought us to such a pass in the most intimate of human relations. It is one of the most extraordinary turns in the social history of mankind that a generation that has made light of the sins of the flesh should nevertheless regard adultery as the unforgivable sin. The idea that a married couple should ever forgive each other this particular sin is regarded as not so much unlikely as un-thinkable. From this springs much of the unhappiness of our times. No one would wish to make light of such sin; but if we had entered more closely into the working of divine atonement, we should never have made such a mistake about our dealings with each other. In marriage, as elsewhere, for-giveness involving complete reconciliation is possible for all who would follow in the footsteps of Christ. And here perhaps more truly than in any other human relations the sorrow of the wounded party may be the start of the other's repentance. When we see the depth of the grief we have caused we must be stony-hearted indeed if we do not wish to make amends, and if we realize that that sorrow is mostly for us who have done the wrong we shall the more easily be moved to repentance.

It is when we think of our relations with God in this way that we realize how inadequate to the human situation are the legal categories of Justice. Sooner or later there must come a time in every life when it is clear that if friendly relations are to be restored the strict demands of justice must be transcended. At any rate as far as the individual is concerned he must throw himself in full contrition on God's mercy, knowing that he cannot, and dare not, plead for simple justice. Shakespeare saw that long ago:

> Therefore, Jew,
> Though justice be thy plea, consider this,
> That in the course of justice none of us
> Should see salvation: we do pray for mercy,
> And that same prayer doth teach us all to render
> The deeds of mercy.

Is then the mere plea for mercy sufficient? Can the claims of justice be entirely ignored? Is Christ's vicarious penitence of itself enough for our salvation, so long as it arouses penitence in us? The answer to these questions is believed to be in the negative. It is not claimed that the aspect of atonement set out in this chapter can ever be taken in isolation. The most that can be claimed for it is that it is valid only in relation with other aspects set out in other chapters. Indeed it may be said that this highly individual approach can only be useful if seen against the wider background of a general change in the relations between God and man.

The individual can claim God's mercy only because accounts between God and man have already been settled by Christ in potentiality. If what we have already said about Jesus' offering of himself as a willing sacrifice has any validity, then the claims of justice have already been satisfied. Consequently man in union with Christ's penitence recognizing his fault may throw himself on God's mercy, asking that he may be included within the sphere of the satisfaction made by Christ.

The theory of vicarious penitence is not contrary to the other aspects of the Atonement. It is complementary to them, and shows how the action they represent may be set in motion for every man who would take advantage of it.

8

Mystical Union

THE aspects of the Atonement we have considered so far have made it appear either as a historical event in the past or else as a legal transaction in the eternal sphere. The aspect we have to consider in this chapter possesses neither of those characteristics but reflects the Atonement as an intimate personal relation here and now.

It is specially intriguing that this aspect should have come into prominent notice at a time when existentialist thinkers have been trying to rescue us from the uncertainties of history and to make the essence of Christianity the encounter of the soul with Christ in the immediate present. We need not, however, share all the current anxieties about the stability of history in order to give due recognition to the immediacy of God's relation with the individual soul. We can be sure of the importance of what God says to each one now without losing sight of what he has said in history. Indeed if we did not have some adequate knowledge of God's revelation of himself in the historic Jesus of Nazareth, we might be hard put to it to recognize the lineaments of the Christ who speaks to us now.

It is particularly necessary to remember this situation when we are dealing with the subject of the Atonement. It would be fatally easy to fall into one of two opposite errors: either to become so engrossed in the historical view as to neglect the point of contact with our own individual soul at the present moment; or to be so lost in the general and eternal truths embodied in the transactional view as to forget the historical fact and so transform our religion into a philosophy.

The aspect of the subject that we put before ourselves in the present chapter is designed to avoid both these dangers. While laying firm hold of the historical events it is intended to keep their effect alive in the present and while grasping the eternal realities to show their relevance in the everyday performance of Christian duties.

Perhaps the best way of introducing this fresh point of view will be to remind ourselves of a pregnant saying of William Law: "What God has done for me is of no value unless it is done in me." Translated into the terms of our present subject that means that no historical event or legal transaction can have any real importance unless it becomes an element of our own experience. This means that all the great acts of God whether in the eternal sphere or on the stage of history must have their echo within the circle of my own personality. It is there and there only that they can be made truly effective for me.

This implies that there is a pervading and lasting character about the specific "acts of God" that does not belong to what we might call the ordinary events of secular history. Of course every event has its effects which cause ripples in the current of time like those caused by a stone thrown into a smooth-running river. They undulate, extend, become fainter until they are lost in the opposing banks. But the acts of God never get lost: they are eternal. They may appear in time, as did the Cross of Calvary, but they reflect a character that is eternal. They stay on: once they are done the world is never the same again: belonging to infinity they can never be repeated but they can reappear in their character and consequences at any given moment in any required context. They are like the sound recordings of some great orchestra heard over the air: they can repeat their music all from one central station simultaneously or at intervals in a million homes.

The all-pervading character of divine events is a favourite

doctrine with St Paul; and he loves to apply it to the sacraments of the Church. These he regards as not separate, isolated acts but as several openings into some great central act which still abides: they are trap-doors into eternity. That is how he sees the relation between baptism and Calvary. When we are baptized we are baptized "into his death" (Rom. 6.3); Those who are baptized have put on Christ (Gal. 3.27). It is noteworthy that St Paul does not find baptism reminds him so much of washing as of death. There is an obvious symbolism of drowning in the ceremony of total immersion. But this was more than stark symbolism. The person thus lowered beneath the water in the name of Jesus was somehow linked with that death upon the cross. He died with Christ to sin and rose again with him to newness of life.

St Paul is so obsessed with this idea of the perpetual continuance of the acts of God done once for all that he seizes the illustration of rabbinic legend to enforce it (1 Cor. 10.1–5). According to the story the rock struck by Moses in the wilderness to provide water for the nomad Israelites rolled along after the wanderers still pouring out its life-giving stream. St Paul gives the story a Christian interpretation: "They drank of that spiritual rock that followed them, and that rock was Christ."

The same essential thought affects the whole theology of St John. Although the Fourth Gospel is as anxious as the Synoptics to insist upon the flesh and blood reality of Christ and the factual actuality of his deeds, it is even more anxious to insist upon the abiding character of everything that was said and done. That is why the doctrine of the Holy Spirit occupies so much larger a proportion of this Gospel. The Spirit is the Spirit of Christ and he will make the presence of Christ an abiding reality: "He will bring all things to your remembrance whatsoever I have said unto you" (14.26); "He shall lead you into all truth" (16.13); "Greater things than these shall he do", who has the power of the Spirit of Christ within him (14.12).

The two sets of teaching are essentially the same. Whether it is Christ himself or Christ in the person of his Spirit the

74

important thing is that he is within us—not far away beyond the farthest star, nor many generations back in history, but here and now within the small and humble circle of our individual personality. Of course the "within" is not to be taken spatially. St Paul indicates his rejection of such crudity by the extraordinary frequency with which he uses the phrase "in Christ", while still being able to speak of "Christ in you" (Col. 1.27). We are reminded of the double metaphor in the Prayer of Humble Access, "that we may evermore dwell in him and he in us". Just as we do not know whether our soul, if it is to be regarded as a separate entity, is in our body or our body in our soul, so we speak paradoxically of Christ being in us at the same time that we think of ourselves as being in him.

This doctrine is prevented from becoming a mere vague pantheistic immanentism by the precise practicality of the sacraments. As baptism ensures a death with Christ and a rising to new life with him, so the Eucharist ensures the continuance and constant refreshment of that new life. This was the appointed means by which in this instance the permanence of God's saving act should be expressed and applied. "As often as ye eat this bread and drink this cup, ye do shew the Lord's death till he come" (1 Cor. 11.26). This is reinforced by the Fourth Gospel, which in its great sixth chapter makes the feeding upon the Lord's Body and Blood the guarantee of eternal life.

It is easily discernible that such teaching can only have realistic value if the character of human personality is very different from what it is usually thought to be. Only too often each person is thought to be cribbed, cabined, and confined within his own being, "each enclosed in his separate ice-palace so that I cannot come to thee nor thou to me". In that case no truly intimate relations between persons are possible and the language used by St Paul and St John becomes merely metaphorical. It is the general opinion of scholars to-day, however, that those New Testament writers meant precisely what they said. It may be felt that what they said was outside the bounds of possibility, but nevertheless, whether they were right or wrong, they really did say in as clear terms as they could use that Christ could and did have an ontological relationship with those who were united to him. There was a mutual interpretation of personality. It is not merely a question of taking up our Cross and following him at a distance, but he is "closer to us than breathing, nearer than hands and feet".

There is further New Testament support for this view. The Fourth Gospel itself records the comparison Jesus made between his own relation to his disciples and that of the vine to its branches. The point of the comparison is that the same sap runs through vine and branches, so that the branch cannot live if it does not draw its interior sustenance from the vine. Similarly the same essential vitality runs through Christ and his disciples. The Christian, to use St Paul's metaphor, is "grafted into" Christ as a twig is grafted into a fruit tree, so that they become part of the same entity. This may seem bold teaching even on the lips of Christ, but there is bolder still in the second epistle of St Peter. There the writer speaks of the special privilege of the Christian as being to be made "partaker of the divine nature". This appears to be the high-water mark of this kind of teaching in the New Testament. It comes out all the more strongly as it occurs quite casually in the greeting of the letter (2 Pet. 1.4).

This is the spring of the so-called deification doctrine, which is found in a number of the early Fathers, particularly those of the eastern Church. The classic expression of it is that given by St Athanasius in his *De Incarnatione*: "God became man in order that we might become God." But it is also found in some of the western Fathers, particularly in St Augustine, "He became partaker of our mortality: he made us partakers of his divinity" (*De Trin.* iv, 1). It might be thought that such teaching could easily have led to a belief that human personality would be eventually absorbed and lost in divinity. But that was never allowed by Christian teachers, at least by those in the main stream of succession. Their caution can be seen in the very similes the mystics used to describe the state of union between the soul and God. The

sponge soaked in the sea and the iron made red-hot in the fire:
these illustrations are employed precisely because neither
sponge nor iron loses its identity when permeated by the
surrounding element of water or fire. So the Christian soul,
when united to God, finds its own individual character en-
hanced rather than destroyed.

> O love that will not let me go
> I give myself anew to thee,
> I pay thee back the life I owe
> That in thine ocean's depths its flow
> May richer, fuller be.

We may seem to have strayed a long way from the thought
of Atonement. But that is not so. It has been necessary to
establish this view of the intimate relations between God and
the individual soul as a genuine part of the Christian tradition
before returning to Law's statement: "What God has done
for me is of no value unless it is also done in me." One cannot
have a satisfactory doctrine of the Atonement unless it is
removed out of the empyrean and out of the pages of history
and brought within the circle of the individual personality.

This doctrine of divine immanence, which fits so neatly
into the historic structure of the sacraments, provides us with
just the bridge we need to cover the gulf between objective
"salvation events" and the soul of the believer. By it we are
enabled to see how the Jesus who lived and taught and died in
first-century Palestine may be a living and vitalizing force in
the individual life to-day. "Christ in me the hope of glory" is
not a bad summary of the doctrine of Atonement thus conceived. It implies that the whole process of redemption, even
if it proceeds independently on the world stage, yet must be
re-enacted in the arena of each human heart.

Actually this is a well-known line of Christian teaching.
It is known as the doctrine of Recapitulation, namely that the
whole history of redemption is summed up in Christ and then
repeated in the life of the believer. It is not without justification from the New Testament. In Eph. 1.10 St Paul speaks of

the dispensation of the fullness of times in which God "might *gather together in one all things in Christ*, both which are in heaven, and which are on earth; even in him: in whom also we have obtained an inheritance, being predestinated according to the purpose of him who worketh all things after the counsel of his own will".

Such a passage must obviously have been dictated with one eye on that "restoration of all things" at the end of the world, of which we hear in St Peter's speeches in Acts. But the words are also intended to convey the thought that within the limited circle of convinced Christians there is already an anticipation of that restoration of all things to their primitive perfection according to the purpose of God. This, of course, is in agreement with the thought of Jesus himself, for he taught that the kingdom of God, whose consummation lies in the future, is nevertheless "among you" or "within you" now. In any case that summing up of all things in Christ and its repetition in the experience of the believer is a regular part of early Christian teaching.

A figure of it may be seen in St Paul's doctrine of the second Adam (Rom. and 1 Cor.). Just as the first Adam was the forerunner of all mankind and summed up all humanity in himself, so Christ was representative man and, being the Word of God incarnate, took the total nature of all mankind upon him. But as all humanity represented in the first Adam had shared in Adam's guilt, so all humanity represented in the second Adam shared in Christ's self-oblation, his death, and his resurrection. It may be said that all history, summed up and spoilt in the first Adam, was summed up again and restored in the second Adam, at least for those who would accept the proffered salvation.

This recapitulation became a favourite doctrine with some of the early Fathers, particularly with Irenaeus towards the end of the second century. H. E. W. Turner in his illuminating lectures on the *Patristic Doctrine of Redemption* distinguishes three elements in Irenaeus' teaching on the subject: restoration, summation, and iteration. Christ, says Irenaeus, recapitulated in himself the long story of mankind. "For this reason although he was perfect he shared the infancy of the children of men, not on his own account, but because of the infancy of man" (*Adv. Haereses,* iv, 63, 1). So he summed up in himself the various ages of man and restored the ancient creation.

It is clear that if this system of salvation is to be effective it must somehow be repeated in the several case of each believer. In what sense can it be repeated? Obviously not in a literal sense because we cannot physically repeat the events of Christ's career: we do not die for others in the way that he did, nor do we expect to appear alive again on this earth a few days after our death and burial. Nevertheless, although repetition does not occur in a literal sense, it still occurs in a real sense.

Jesus is born again in us when we turn to him by faith and are made members of his body, an event that is typified and sealed in baptism. His death is renewed in us when we die to sin. "God forbid that I should glory, save in the cross of our Lord Jesus Christ, by whom the world is crucified unto me, and I unto the world" (Gal. 6.14). He rises again in us when we turn from the darkness of a life lived for selfish ends and set ourselves to face the light of the new life to be lived in him. And that new life, which is really his more than ours, will be exercised by daily godliness of living and nourished by frequent participation in the "breaking of bread". So will Christ grow to maturity in us.

It is sometimes suggested that any satisfaction we might feel in this presentation of the more mystical theory of the Atonement is marred by the fact that it lays so little emphasis on the *moral* claims of Christianity. Surely the purpose of our religion is to produce ethical goodness: then why do we hear so little about it in this method of explaining the means of our salvation? We would answer that in fact the primary purpose of religion is not to produce moral goodness, but to put us in the right relation with God. From that relation moral goodness should flow. Certainly no one should ever imagine that he can be in the right relation with God if he is not aiming constantly at amendment of life (1 John 3.3). But the amendment is the result of the contact with God, not its cause. Christ does not wait until we have amended our lives before he offers atonement for us—"God commendeth his own love toward us in that while we were yet sinners Christ died for us" (Rom. 5.8); "We love him because he first loved us" (John 4.19).

Having died for us he communicates himself to us. Here he is, in all the freshness of his risen life, indeed a well of water springing up to everlasting life. The barriers are down: we are one with God: the life of his Son within us expresses itself as far as we will let it in the beauty, wisdom, and strength of everyday Christian living. Here is all the moral goodness we can ever need, or ever hope for, waiting to express itself in our own thoughts and words and deeds. He will indeed speak with our lips, look through our eyes, work with our hands until we can say with St Paul, "It is no longer I that live but Christ that liveth in me" (Gal. 2.20). This is the fruit of that mystical union between Christ and the believer without which the doctrine of the Atonement would lose half its force.

9

The Atonement To-day

THE time has now come when we must sum up what we have discovered so far about the various interpretations of the Atonement and ask ourselves what meaning the total doctrine has for us to-day.

The preliminary difficulty is that so many people fail to see any need for it at all. A liberal Jew, trying to show why for him the Christian doctrine of Atonement seemed altogether unnecessary, explained that if we really believed that God was love then all we needed to realize was that as soon as we are sorry for our faults then God's arms are immediately open to us. And he cited the parable of the prodigal son as an example of the fact that that was really the true Christian teaching.

Of course it is. We remember the Collect for Ash Wednesday:

> Almighty and everlasting God, who hatest nothing that thou hast made, and dost forgive the sins of all them that are penitent: Create and make in us new and contrite hearts, that we worthily lamenting our sins, and acknowledging our wretchedness, may obtain of thee, the God of all mercy, perfect remission and forgiveness; through Jesus Christ our Lord.

Actually we can go further than this and say that the divine arms are always open to us. The initiative does not lie with us, for God has already taken it: "While we were yet sinners Christ died for us" (Rom. 5.8). It is the recognition of this fact that in countless instances has broken down the stubborn resistance of the sinner and made him first realize the true nature of his sin. This aspect of the situation has been well expressed in the saying that the New Testament revelation is an offer not only of "forgiveness to those who repent but of repentance to those who sin".

As soon as we are sorry the natural instinct is to throw ourselves into the arms of the Father, certain that we shall not be rebuffed. But what makes us so certain, and what indeed makes it possible and proper for God to act in that way? These are the questions the doctrine of the Atonement is designed to answer. We know from our human experience that mere indulgence is no answer. Simply to ignore sin may allow an act to become a habit and a habit to develop into a character. Whatever reconciliation there is must, therefore, take account of the wrong committed.

It is our contention that the Atonement justified the immediate access of the penitent to the Father. One does not shrink from the inference that in this sense it inaugurated a new covenant, a new system of relations between God and man. It was actually a turning point in history. Before it the chosen people had been taught to approach God under cover of the Law. That Law had gone through various stages of development, but common to all of them alike was the notion of sacrifice. In the Christian dispensation its place was taken by Christ. He was the one mediator between God and man, and the one sacrifice offered for the sins of the whole world. Whereas in the old dispensation man could only come before God with a gift, under the new dispensation his characteristic thought became, "Nothing in my hand I bring".

It is of the essence of mediation that it points in two directions. Mediation between God and man has often been described in terms of a two-way traffic, descending and ascending. Certainly both Old and New Testaments are concerned to keep the subject of mediation in the forefront of their teaching. Thus in the Old Testament God approaches man through angels and Moses and the Law, while man approaches God through Moses, Jeremiah, Ezekiel, and the Suffering Servant (Isa. 53), to say nothing of the whole order of priesthood.

To these intermediaries we have to add in late Judaism the figure of Wisdom. The semi-hypostatized virtue gives its name to a whole type of literature, the Wisdom Literature, which, starting from Proverbs and Job, comes to its full flower in Ecclesiasticus and Wisdom. What prevents wisdom from becoming an entirely satisfactory representative of God is that it is generally pictured as a female figure. Nevertheless it serves to keep the idea of personal mediation open until the period of the New Testament.

There at last the mediator is fully identified with the person of Christ. In him the descending and ascending aspects of mediation are combined. Christ is God's representative to man: "If ye had known me, ye would have known my Father also" (John 14.7). As perfect man he is also man's representative to God: "We have not a high priest who is unable to sympathize with our weaknesses, but one who in every respect has been tempted as we are, yet without sinning" (Heb. 14.15). Thus the Epistle to the Hebrews sees the whole work of mediation now concentrated in Christ as once it had been in the Jewish priesthood.

The double aspect of Christ's mediation must thus have formed part of the earliest apostolic tradition. It certainly continued on into the Apostolic Fathers and beyond. To the early Alexandrians like Clement and Origen Jesus was above all the Illuminator who revealed the nature and the ways of God to man. To Irenaeus he was the Victor who recapitulated in himself the whole activity of God in respect of man. To Ignatius, the martyr-bishop of Antioch, he was the Giver of immortality, "the antidote that we should not die". To all alike he was the Victim, offered by himself on behalf of the erring children of men. Because of his perfection in two natures he was able to deal on equal terms with both God and man, and thus to make complete reconciliation between them.

It would be a mistake to think of this reconciliation as being effected by one single action, however dramatic and striking. It is true that it might come to a head in such an event, as the rays from the sun can be gathered together and applied to one spot by means of a glass. So the Cross will always stand out as the special *locus* of the Atonement. But there is a double penumbra of that Cross on Calvary that must be always borne in mind. There is first the earthly life of Christ exercising its reconciling influence in every word and deed. And there is also the eternal love of God, pursuing in infinity its predestined plan for men, of which this event on Calvary is the historic expression. As Keats in his "Ode on a Grecian Urn" saw eternal reality caught in a moment of time, "For ever wilt thou love and she be fair", so the Cross has caught for us throughout all time the image of the self-sacrificing love of God. The Atonement itself, however, is not a once-for-all historical event but the permanent action of the reconciling love of God, exhibited in the work and teaching, the resurrection and ascension of Christ, in the descent of the Spirit, and in the continuing life of the Church.

By the same token our perception and acceptance of the offer of reconciliation may be instantaneous, but it must pervade all our life. The conviction may come suddenly in a blinding flash of realization or it may dawn slowly upon our consciousness, so slowly in fact that we cannot tell when it first began. But it is there, and once it is recognized there is not an element or aspect of life that is not affected by it. It is the "contact lens" through which we look out upon the whole of our surroundings. We can now see clearly, whereas everything before was dim and distorted. We are in tune not only with the Infinite but with all the circumstances of daily life.

It is to be remarked also that the reconciliation is both individual and universal, that is to say that, while it applies to each person distinctly and must be accepted by each on his own behalf, at the same time it is to be seen as affecting the created world of men and things as a whole, as a cosmos, as an ordered universe. It is a witness to the redeemability of man's culture, his art, his language, his science, his industry—everything in fact which now shows the contamination of his sin. That is what is affirmed in Col. 1.19: "God willed that in Christ the plenitude of Deity should have its abode, and that through him he should reconcile the universe to himself. This God has done by making the blood of his Cross the means of establishing peace, so effecting through him a restoration of all things both in earth and heaven."[1]

Although the initiative comes from God, he does not disdain to use human ministers to effect the reconciliation. So St Paul tells the Corinthians: "Everything comes from God, who has reconciled us to himself through Christ, and has committed to me the ministry of reconciliation. That ministry is based on the fact that God was in Christ reconciling the world to himself, wiping out the debit balance of our transgressions and setting his reconciliation to the credit of our account."[2]

This is a sufficient warrant for the Church's ministry of reconciliation. But it is nothing like so strong as the statement in the Gospels, "Whosoever sins ye remit they are remitted unto them, and whosoever sins ye retain they are retained" (John 20.23). In any case there was evidently a secure element in the apostolic tradition that, although God himself bestowed reconciliation on such as were willing to receive it, the Church and its officers were the chosen instruments for applying it to the consciences of men.

One might ask what were expected to be the results of this reconciliation in the everyday life and character of the individual. A complete answer would be, "all the graces of the Christian life". We might content ourselves with saying that from this established point of contact all the rest flows: the soul once reconciled to God is the recipient of every grace and favour that it shows itself capable of assimilating. Nevertheless there is advantage in trying to be more specific and in endeavouring to enumerate the distinctive results that may be expected.

[1] Translated in Wand: *New Testament Letters*, p. 106.
[2] Op. cit., p. 60. 2 Cor. 5.18.

First, there is the fellowship that is now set up with both God and man through Christ. So St Paul can tell the Corinthians that Christ is the only ground of assurance, but that in him they have now found all the wisdom, holiness, and righteousness of God. At the same time the ardent nature of Paul's own fellowship with other Christians is shown in the fact that he can call the Philippians his "joy and crown", and can tell the Thessalonians that he "really feels alive again" now that he has been assured of their loyalty and love (Phil. 4.1; 1 Thess. 3.8).

Secondly, the consciousness of fellowship with God deepens into a sense of sonship: "The spirit you received was not a slavish spirit so that you should again fall into a condition of terror, but you received the filial spirit which enables us to address God confidently as Father" (Rom. 8.15). Paul is even more explicit with the Galatians: "When the right moment arrived, God sent his Son, born by means of a human birth and consequently subject to the Law, to redeem those who were subject to the Law, in order that we might be made his sons by adoption. And once you became his sons God sent the Spirit of his Son into your hearts to give expression to the fact of your sonship by addressing him as 'Our Father'. So then you are no longer servants but sons, and if sons then also heirs—so constituted by God himself" (Gal. 4.5). In Ephesians this adoption is seen as part of God's eternal plan: "In his love he foreordained us through Jesus Christ to adoption into his family" (1.5).

Thirdly, such a relationship with God, the All-Holy, is intended to result in our sanctification. St Paul sees two lives in strongly contrasted terms and gives lists of the virtues that distinguish the one and the vices that distinguish the other (Gal. 5). More generally while the latter state is characterized as a condition of slavery dominated by fear, the former is infused by the spirit of sonship which enables us to address even the eternal Majesty by an endearing name (Rom. 8.15). St Peter says we have been consecrated by the Spirit so as to become obedient to Jesus Christ, by the sprinkling of whose blood we have entered into fellowship with God (1 Pet. 1.2).

St John says that because we are God's children we have a hope of one day being like him, and because we have that hope we set about practising a life of purity here and now (1 John 3.3).

We thus see that the Atonement is expected to result in reconciliation with God here in this life, and that reconciliation will show itself in moral goodness now and in visible unity with him in the life hereafter. That is what is deemed to be the *fact* of the Atonement: all the various *theories* are intended to show how as a matter of history it came about and how the act of God by which it was accomplished was in accordance with the general fitness of things and in line with a true moral order. It is natural that as our experience grows and our understanding deepens these views should change from time to time and demand some measure of restatement. "When I was a child I thought as a child, but when I became a man I put away childish things."

It is manifest that some of the views we have discussed, such as the trick by which the devil was deceived, belong to the childhood of the race. Others, like the picture of the law court and even the age-long ritual of sacrifice, are more sophisticated, but still belong to the world of symbolism. Whether it is possible to explain the doctrine without some sort of symbol may very well be doubted. But that need not trouble us. We do most of our thinking by means of symbols, and the fact that even God is sometimes spoken of as a symbol does not mean that he does not exist, but that our idea of God points to something beyond itself still more true and inexpressible.

The actual crucifixion is generally accepted as one of the securest facts of history. The Christian Faith sees it as something which did not begin and end in time but as an event also in the eternal sphere permanently affecting the relations between God and man. The various theories of the Atonement are attempts to show how this fitted into God's scheme of things and how by it the moral order of the universe was not abrogated but transcended. It can never be easy to explain how mercy can be at the same time just and above justice, and in any case each generation seems to have its own idea of what justice is. It is the merit of the various theories outlined in the present volume that each of them adds a little to our knowledge of what a complete answer must include.

Roughly speaking, they fall into three classes, historical, legal, and personal. Under the first heading would be included the exemplarist and the victory concepts; under the second the substitution, transaction, and satisfaction theories; under the last the ideas of vicarious penitence and mystical union. The three classes are not mutually exclusive, and to some extent they overlap; but in the main they exhibit three different interests.

Both the exemplarist and the victory theories lay special emphasis on the historical event of the crucifixion. What happened in Palestine in the first century A.D. is of fundamental importance: without it there could have been no reconciliation. It is true that neither view stops at the historical incident. The exemplarist jumps straight from the event on Calvary to the challenge made by Christ to the conscience of the individual here and now. The *Christ Victor* theory thinks not only of the victory on the Cross but also of the defeat of the demons, the harrowing of hell, the resurrection, and the conquests made by the Church down the centuries. But all alike stem from Calvary. The historical event is kept to the fore. It is indeed well that in all ages we should be led to keep our gaze upon the Cross.

The three middle views are more concerned with what happens in the empyrean. They reflect mostly the courts of heaven and the eternal character of justice. They are interested in essential questions of right and wrong. In the long run they have to admit that you cannot properly consider justice merely as an isolated ideal. It is concerned with real people, flesh and blood, actual personalities; and what is personal does not easily submit itself to precise logical or mathematical demonstration. Whatever may be the logic or the justice of it, in everyday life men and women do offer themselves as sacrifices for others: substitution is a common fact, and we

88

all know that the world would be infinitely poorer if it were not so.

These ideas must somehow have a place in God's plan; but the restless mind of man will never be completely at ease so long as he fails to find some way of reconciling them with the eternal justice of God. This is what the three theories of transaction, sacrifice, and substitution attempt to do. Whether we accept them as completely valid or not, their main value for us to-day is that they preserve for us the belief in the absolute importance of the issues between right and wrong. They make it impossible for us to think lightly of the moral law. But when rightly understood they suffuse it with the guarantee of God's love and make us sure that there is a proper place for self-sacrifice and substitution in our own lives.

The theories that are most personal in the sense that they bring the Atonement closest to our hearts are those of vicarious penitence and mystical union. They belong very close together. The thought of Jesus' sorrow for me as he hung upon the cross is intensely moving, but it is not likely to be effective unless it stirs up genuine penitence in my own heart. And how can that penitence be better stirred than by the thought that Christ is already being sorry in me? Since we are joined together I need not look for a proper feeling of penitence outside myself in order to bring it within to act for me. Christ is already there in all his vicarious penitence and what I have to do is to let his sorrow flood my heart. The Christ in me identifies himself with the Jesus of history, and the atonement made once and for all for the sins of the whole world is applied to my own case.